MW01539406

The tourist's companion, or the history and antiquities of Harewood, in Yorkshire, giving a particular description of Harewood House, Church and Castle, etc. [With a pedigree of the family of Lascelles.]

John Jewell

The tourist's companion, or the history and antiquities of Harewood, in Yorkshire, giving a particular description of Harewood House, Church and Castle, etc. [With a pedigree of the family of Lascelles.]

Jewell, John
British Library, Historical Print Editions
British Library
1819
85 p. ; 8°.
10352.b.37.

The BiblioLife Network

This project was made possible in part by the BiblioLife Network (BLN), a project aimed at addressing some of the huge challenges facing book preservationists around the world. The BLN includes libraries, library networks, archives, subject matter experts, online communities and library service providers. We believe every book ever published should be available as a high-quality print reproduction; printed on- demand anywhere in the world. This insures the ongoing accessibility of the content and helps generate sustainable revenue for the libraries and organizations that work to preserve these important materials.

The following book is in the "public domain" and represents an authentic reproduction of the text as printed by the original publisher. While we have attempted to accurately maintain the integrity of the original work, there are sometimes problems with the original book or micro-film from which the books were digitized. This can result in minor errors in reproduction. Possible imperfections include missing and blurred pages, poor pictures, markings and other reproduction issues beyond our control. Because this work is culturally important, we have made it available as part of our commitment to protecting, preserving, and promoting the world's literature.

GUIDE TO FOLD-OUTS, MAPS and OVERSIZED IMAGES

In an online database, page images do not need to conform to the size restrictions found in a printed book. When converting these images back into a printed bound book, the page sizes are standardized in ways that maintain the detail of the original. For large images, such as fold-out maps, the original page image is split into two or more pages.

Guidelines used to determine the split of oversize pages:

• Some images are split vertically; large images require vertical and horizontal splits.
• For horizontal splits, the content is split left to right.
• For vertical splits, the content is split from top to bottom.
• For both vertical and horizontal splits, the image is processed from top left to bottom right.

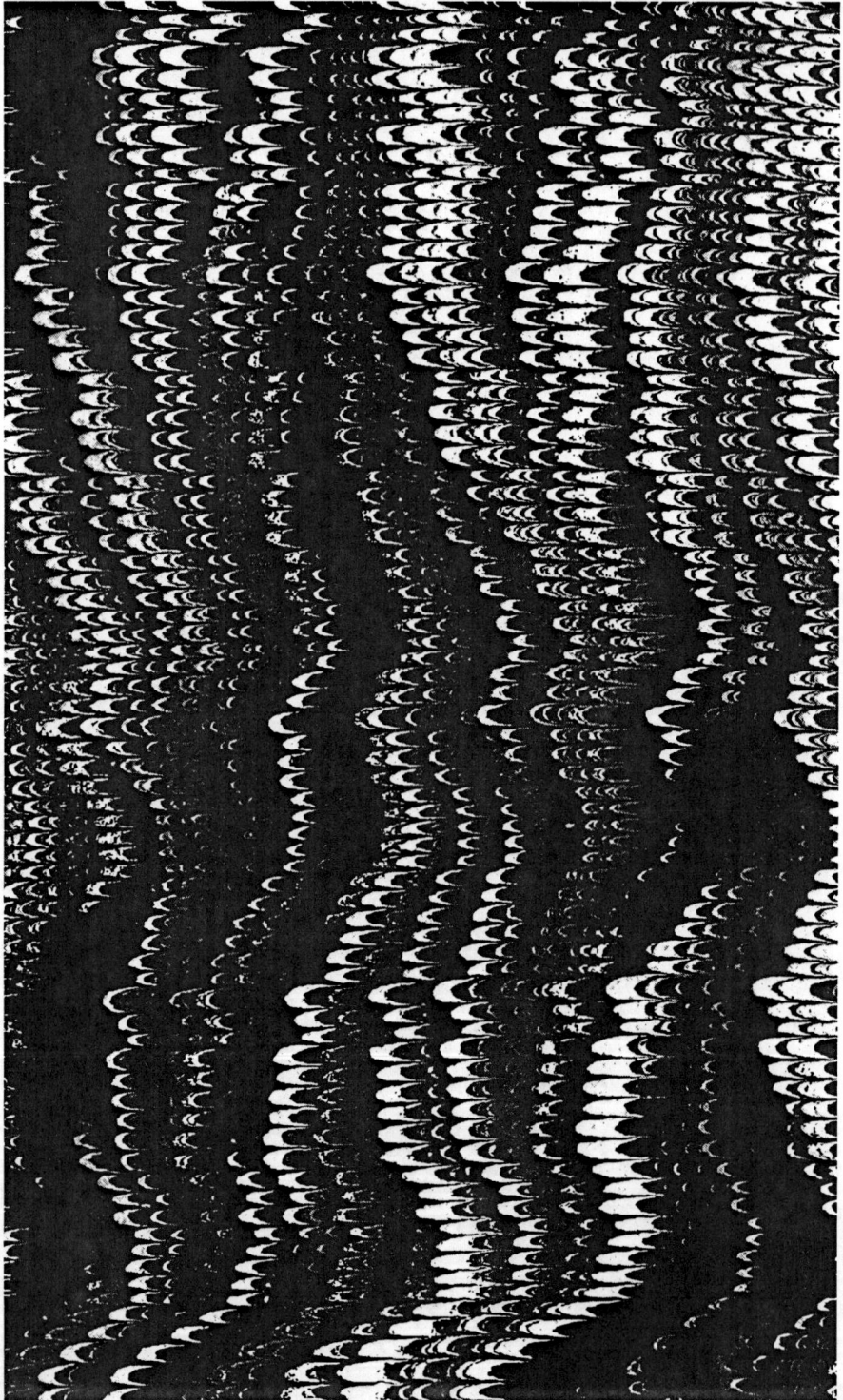

. Perfect

a scarce very ypbrime
- Book

BRITISH
MUSEUM

S.E. VIEW of HAREWOOD HOUSE YORKSHIRE.
The Seat of the Right Hon.ble Earl Harewood

THE
TOURIST'S COMPANION,

OR THE

HISTORY

AND

ANTIQUITIES

OF

HAREWOOD,

IN YORKSHIRE,

GIVING A PARTICULAR DESCRIPTION OF

Harewood House, Church, and Castle:

WITH SOME ACCOUNT OF ITS ENVIRONS, SELECTED
FROM VARIOUS AUTHORS, AND CONTAINING
MUCH INFORMATION NEVER BEFORE
PUBLISHED.

BY JOHN JEWELL.

——◦❦◦——

LEEDS:

PRINTED BY B. DEWHIRST, AND SOLD BY THE BOOK-
SELLERS AT LEEDS, HARROGATE, OTLEY, &c.

——

1819.

INTRODUCTION.

---◇---

Candid Reader,

This Work was not originally intended for publication, but was merely the amusement of leisure hours, but through persuasion I scarcely know how to resist; I now offer it to the public, solely from a hope of its being found, in some degree, useful, yet with all the imperfections of a writer, unaccustomed to compose for the press, I hope (with the aid of other authors) it may have the good effect of engaging the attention of an abler pen.

I can only hope, that this small work may be considered as some guide or amusement, to the lovers of natural curiosities, in their researches. Under this predicament, we may amuse ourselves and others; but I am sorry, the history of antient times, is enveloped so much in shade, that it is difficult to trace with precision, the remote origin of places, and, in the elucidation of subjects of this nature, the mind is too frequently led astray by the delusive excursions of fancy; but I have been as concise in the description as possible, retaining their original names and characters, and explaining myself in as easy and familiar a manner as I was able.

Should the intelligent reader in scanning over this work, discover any errors, of which doubtless there are some, the Author will feel it a special act of kindness, if he will communicate them, in order that they may be corrected in another edition, should it be called for.

Harewood, July, 1819.

HAREWOOD.

THIS beautiful village is situated on the summit
of a hill, on the road from Leeds to Harrogate,
about eight miles from each place, eight miles
east of Otley, seven miles west of Wetherby,
twenty-one from York, and one hundred and
ninety-nine miles and a half north by north-west
of London.

Harewood may be distinguished from almost
every other village in the kingdom, by its regu-
larity and cleanliness. The whole town consists
principally of two streets, one running north and
south, the other east and west; the first fronting
the road from Leeds to Harrogate, the latter the
road from Wetherby, forming a regular approach
to the gateway, leading to Harewood House,
has been uniformly and modestly rebuilt, so as
to exclude every appearance of filth or poverty.
The whole of the town is built with fine stone,
procured from the neighbouring quarries, and
even the cottages possess a look of neatness
bordering upon elegance, while the principal
houses assume an air of superiority, that accords
with the vast domain to which they appertain,
and reflect the highest praise to the liberal mind
which erected them.

We shall here quote the words of an elegant
writer on topography, Dr. Whitaker, who says,

"This is a fortunate place, blessed with much natural beauty and fertility, and, in the compass of a country village, with an entire though dismantled castle, a modern palace surrounded by a wide extent of pleasure grounds and plantations, and a parish church filled with unmutilated sculptures of the fourteenth and fifteenth centuries."

The population of Harewood including Bondgate, (of which more hereafter) in March 1818, was 854, and the inhabitants are principally composed of farmers, shopkeepers, artisans, and labourers; the latter of whom are constantly employed by the Earl of Harewood, in either one situation or another, for to this village manufacture is a stranger, and, perhaps, many of its concomitant vices. About the year 1755, the late Lord Harewood built a range of houses to the right of the entrance from Wetherby, and established a ribbon manufactory, but it was of short duration, as it was discontinued about 1766.

The soil about Harewood is of various qualities, but in general, fine arable, and good pasture land, particularly in Wharfdale.

In 1814 his Lordship apportioned a considerable quantity of good pasture and arable land, to the cottagers, for gardens, and those who best cultivate their portions, receive great encouragement. Is not this worthy of imitation and admiration?

In the year 1208, king John granted to Warren Fitzgerald, his chamberlain, a charter for a fair at this place, to be held on the first day of July and two following days; at present they are held on the last Monday in April, and second Monday in October; also a charter for a market, which is held every monday morning, for calves, sheep, &c. and it is not many years since corn and other produce were brought here for sale in great abundance, of late, however, the market has very much decayed, probably from its nearness to the more populous towns of Leeds, Otley, Wetherby, and Knaresborough.

MARKET CROSS.

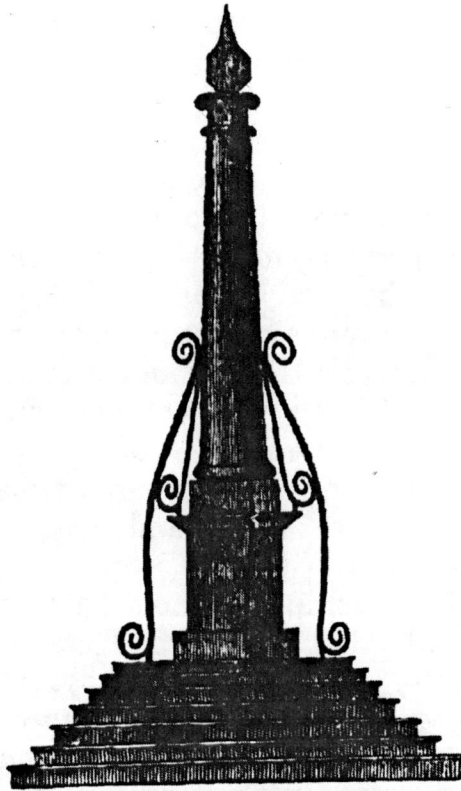

About three parts up the street running east to west, and towards Leeds, stood the market cross, made of fine stone, surrounded by steps. It was taken down July 14th, 1804, and the author has been at considerable trouble, in obtaining the annexed representation.

The parish of Harewood is partly in the wapentake of Claro, and extends in both divisions of Skyrac. It has eight dependent constableries, the population of which were enumerated, with much care, under the direction of the Vicar, the Rev Richard Hale, in the year 1808, as follows,

The township of Harewood, - - 809
Alwoodley, - - 128
Wigton, - - - 156
Wike, - - - 42
Weardley, - - 166
Weeton, - - 300
Dunkeswick, - 249
Eastkeswick, - 256

Total 2106

When the population was taken, the 27th of May, 1818, they were as follows.

Harewood, - - 854
Alwoodley, - 149
Wigton, - - 163
Wike, - - - 48
Weardley, - - 173
Weeton, - - 305
Dunkeswick, - 233
Eastkeswick, - 279

Total 2214

Increase in ten years, 108

THE COURT,

The Right Honourable the Earl of Harewood, calls his court leet, and court baron, twice a year, about Easter and Michaelmas, in the school-room, where the inhabitants meet, to which they owe suit and service, and all actions under forty shillings are determined; here also the constables and other parish officers attend, to be sworn into office, for their respective townships.

THE SCHOOL.

This school was built about 1771, by the late Lord Harewood. In charitable institutions, the village of Harewood may boast, a particular attention being paid to the aged, and to the infant poor. The present Earl of Harewood is very generous and charitable, is a considerable bene- factor to the church, and poor of his parish ; for ever since he came to this estate, he hath allowed a considerable sum to cloathe eight singing boys every Christmas, and another to his principal musician and church choristers, likewise to a schoolmaster in the town, to teach the poor children reading, writing, and arithmetic, gratis. The number of free scholars in the year 1819, was as follows.

The Earl of Harewood, - - - 20 boys.
Viscount Lascelles, - - - - 12 do.
Viscountess Lascelles, - - - 14 girls.
The Honourable Miss Lascelles, 2 do.

INNS.

The Harewood Arms is the only inn * in the village (before which the public road passes) where the company may refresh themselves, and leave their horses, while they survey the scenes herein described. The house is nearly new, and has been fitted up in a neat and commodious manner; the rooms are well furnished with new beds and bedding, the cellars are well stored with liquors; good post-chaise, able horses, and careful drivers, are at command.

COACH.

The Telegraph coach goes through Harewood, every morning, about six o'clock, in its way from Leeds to Sunderland, and returns the same evening about seven o'clock, on its way to Leeds. This village is well provided with carriers, to all parts of the country; the Skipton carrier goes through every Tuesday, on his way to York, and returns on Thursday.

THE POST

Comes into this village every morning about three o'clock, (Tuesday excepted from London) goes out to all parts the same evening at six o'clock.—Wetherby is the post town for Harewood.

---

* About forty years since, there were six public houses in this village, the White Hart, (then the head inn) Black Bull, Shoulder of Mutton, Red Lion, Crown, and the Star. Two at Lofthouse, two at Weardley, one at Weeton, one at Dunkeswick, and one at the Bridge.

LASCELLES, EARL OF HAREWOOD.

Arms: Sable, a Cross patonce within a Border, Or. Crest: on a Wreath a Bear's Head couped, Ermine; muzzled, Gules, gorged with a Collar of the last, studded and rimmed, Or. Supporters: two Bears, Ermine; each muzzled, Gules, gorged with a Collar of the second, rimmed, studded and Chain refixed over the Back. Or: a pendant thereto an Escutcheon, sable, charged with a Cross patonce of the third, Or.

HAREWOOD HOUSE.

The magnificent and princely residence of the Right Honourable the Earl of Harewood. The entrance to the park is joining to the village, by a most superb arched gateway of the Doric order, with two dwellings; the first stone was laid December 1801. Here are eight noble columns, twenty feet high, seventeen feet of which are solid stone. This magnificent piece of workmanship does great credit to the architect, the late Mr. Carr, of York; likewise to the mason, the late Mr. John Muschamp, of Harewood: at a small distance, and at the end of some very strong pallisadoing, are two small pavilions, to correspond with the gateway, at the back of which, on the walls, are two talbots. The whole together, is so uniform with the village, that it forms one of the most elegant entrances in the kingdom.

On entering the park, of about one thousand eight hundred acres of exceeding good pasture land, it cannot be expressed the great variety it affords, of hills, and dales, thick woods and scattered groves, which strike the eye with a most picturesque, and ever-varying effect.

> Here flocks and herds in pastures rove,
> Here range the songsters of the grove;
> Here do the lark and linnet sing,
> And hail the kind return of spring.

On the right, going down the park, is a south-east view of the church, intersected by the pleasure grounds, of which, I shall give a description in its proper place, and proceed on through a cluster of old trees, called the oaks, to the beautiful mansion, the seat of the Right Hon. the Earl of Harewood, which is about three-quarters of a mile west of the village, and stands on a fine eminence, sheltered from the north and west winds, by the pleasure grounds, as in the frontispiece.

It is so justly celebrated for its beauty, grandeur of style, elegance of decoration and finishing, both externally and internally, that it is deservedly ranked with the first buildings in the kingdom. It was built by the late Right Hon. Lord Harewood, who laid the first stone of the foundation, at the south-east corner, March 23d, 1759,—The designs was made by the late Mr. Carr of York, and Mr. Adams of London ; the late Mr. John Muschamp, of Harewood, was the mason. The whole length of the building is two hundred and forty-eight feet, six inches, the width eighty-five feet, the height from the flags, sixty-two feet.

The wings of the north front are enriched with emblematical medallions, representing Liberty, Britannia, Agriculture, and Commerce; executed in a masterly manner by Collins, from the designs of Zucchi; in the centre is a handsome pediment, supported by six three-quarter Corinthian columns, thirty feet high, which compose the entrance, from a flight of eight steps, fifty-two feet in length, guarded by two Sphinxes,* exe-

---

* The Sphinx was a supposed monster, of upper Egypt ; near the city of Thebes, having the face and voice of a

cuted by Richardson, of Doncaster; on the top of these steps are some very large flags, well worthy of notice, nine feet ten inches in length, and seven feet nine inches in width. From this front is seen Alms-Cliff,* about four miles distance, through an opening in the pleasure grounds to the left, made for that purpose; over a fertile vale, intersected by the river Wharfe. To the right, about four hundred and thirty-nine yards distance, through another opening, the eye is gratified with a rich treat of scenery, enlivened by the parish church, the walls of which, at the west end, are covered with ivy, quite to the top of the steeple.

This noble mansion, on the outside, claims every merit of Corinthian architecture. The body is well proportioned, and joined by two superb wings. The fine stone of which it is built, was dug from a quarry near the place. Here is a large area, eight feet six inches in width, and eleven feet in height, which extends the whole length of the north front, and is well secured with stong iron palisadoes, ornamented with eight beautiful lamps. In crossing this

---

woman, the body like a dog, the tail of a dragon, and claws of a lion, they infested the city of Thebes, proposing questions to those that passed by; and if they could not previously resolve them, it devoured them without mercy. They were likewise put to signify mysteries, at the entrance of all the tables of Egypt.

* Alms-Cliff, it is said, derived its name from the distribution of alms, at certain stated times, agreeable to the tenor of legacies left to the chapel which stood there in the sixteenth century, and was at that time dedicated to the Virgin Mary.—Watts's Views.—Where the chapel stood, now goes by the name of Chapel Hill.

area, are all the coal-offices, &c. quite under ground.

This south front hath still superior excellence, and is adorned with a Tetrastyle Corinthian portico and pediment, supported by four elegant columns, thirty feet three inches high, and nine feet eight inches in circumference, upon a handsome rustic basement, which is continued round the whole building, and the wings terminate in a Corinthian pilastrade.

The ground, which was originally a rough hill, is now sweetly sloped with great art and judgment, from whence the eye is led to a spacious sheet of thirty-two acres of water, gently winding in a serpentine course, beyond which, the country forms one of the most beautiful, and picturesque scenes imaginable. I may say with the poet,

> —— —— —Who can paint
> Like nature? Can imagination boast,
> Amid its gay creation, hues like these?
> Or can it mix them with that matchless skill,
> And lose them in each other, as appears
> In every bud that blows?

Through every part of this princely mansion, elegance and usefulness are evidently united; and, though nothing can exceed the work of the mason, the carver, the painter, and the upholsterer; it is at the same time, a most complete and useful family residence. It was first inhabited, in the year 1771.

The above described seat, is open to the public every Saturday, from eleven o'clock in the morning, until four o'clock in the afternoon; of which obliging permission, the nobility and gentry who frequent Harrogate, avail themselves much, the short distance forming a most agreeable excursion.

ENTRANCE HALL.

A magnificent room of the Doric order, forty feet four inches, by thirty-one feet five inches, nineteen feet two inches high; lately fitted up in the Egyptian style, here are some elegant Grecian stools and chairs, eight two-arm chairs with the family crest on them; twelve elegant fluted columns, and four pilasters in the corners, highly painted, resembling porphyry marble, the walls are resembling siena marble, by Mr. Hutchinson of London. The pannels on the walls, are richly adorned with trophies of war, &c. by Rose. Here are six niches, wherein are placed the following bronzed statues, viz. a Bachante, Flora, Night, Minerva, Iris, and Euterpe, under the dome are two small niches, in them are two beautiful urns. Over the two fire-places are the triumphs of Mars and Neptune, by Collins. From the centre of the ceiling, is suspended a beautiful lamp, under which, is an elegant slab of dove marble, six feet by three feet six inches, on a Grecian frame.

LIBRARY.

Thirty feet by twenty-two feet six inches, nineteen feet two inches high. The ceiling terminates in a cove, richly ornamented, and supported by eighteen pilasters with Corinthian capitals; elegantly fitted up with about four thousand books, in most languages, arts, and sciences. Here is a billiard table, and two glass frames, wherein are some models of the French flotilla, and a seventy-four gun ship; in the niches above, are the following busts, viz.

Newton, Machiavel, Dante, Petrarch, Boccacio, and Sappho. The following paintings over the chimney-piece, by Rebecca, are the Sacrifice of Homer, in Fresco, and a beautiful painting of Minerva and other goddesses. In the pannels on the walls, are two historical paintings, and four of Pliny, educating his daughter, in one of which, she is weeping for the loss of her bird, while he is writing the ode for it.

> " No more this little warbler's throat,
> Will e'er expand its thrilling note ;
> Or charm away a tedious hour,
> With silver sounds of dulcet pow'r.
> Its notes are lost, its beauty's fled,
> And here the songster rests his head.

LITTLE LIBRARY.

Eighteen feet by fourteen feet five inches, fourteen feet seven inches high; contains some elegant book-cases, over the fire-place is the ceremonies of an antique marriage, by Collins, and four other figures on the walls.

PASSAGE.

Twenty-three feet six inches, by six feet six inches, thirteen feet five inches high; contains oil paintings of favourite dogs, also maps, &c.

THE EARL OF HAREWOOD'S DRESSING-ROOM.

Twenty-four feet three inches, by eighteen feet nine inches, fourteen feet nine inches high; over the chimney-piece is an elegant looking-glass, seven feet six inches by four feet eleven inches ; two beautiful mahogany presses, on the top of which, are Shakspeare, Milton, Pope, and Johnson ; eight views of foreign sea-ports, and the following portraits, viz. His Grace the Duke of Wellington, the late Right Honourable Wm. Pitt, the Right Honourable the Viscountess Lascelles, and Miss Hale, by Edridge ; the late Lady Harewood, Marquis Cornwallis, General Phipps, and two others ; also hunting pieces ; over the doors in pyrography, by Mr. Smith of Skipton Castle, are the Orphans, and Simeon with the infant Christ in his arms. —See Luke ii 25—36.

COUCH OR BATH ROOM.

Twenty-five feet six inches, by eleven feet eight inches, and fourteen feet ten inches high. Over the doors are the portraits of the late Lord Harewood, and his first wife ; besides two large oval looking-glasses.

BLUE ROOM.

Twenty-one feet seven inches, by fifteen feet three inches, fourteen feet eight inches high ; the furniture crimson and gold, an elegant gilt four-post bedstead, hung with crimson damask ; on the top is a stork. Here is a picture of the late Lady Frances Douglas, by Sir Joshua Reynolds, and another over the fire-place con-tains some of her Ladyship's children by the same master. On the chimney-piece is Sappho writing her ode, dictated by Love.—Indian figures, &c.

EARL OF HAREWOOD's BED-ROOM.

Twenty-six feet three inches, by twenty feet nine inches, fourteen feet nine inches high. The furniture blue and gold, the walls are hung with French paper; here is an elegant cabinet, and a variety of Indian figures, &c. This room commands beautiful views into the flower-garden, and south front of the house.

ANTI ROOM.

Eighteen feet three inches, by ten feet seven inches, fourteen feet one inch high : This room contains a beautiful sham library, by Mr. Fryer, and an elegant portrait of one Jane Birdsall, with a fowl under her left arm, picking corn out of her right hand.—This woman was accused of magical arts.

STATE BED ROOM.

Twenty seven feet one inch, by eighteen feet six inches, fifteen feet five inches high, the furniture green and gold; the bed and the room is hung with green damask, bordered with gold; the bed is placed under a rich canopy, supported by columns of the Ionic order. Over a most beautiful ornamented chimneypiece of white marble, is an elegant Indian glass, adorned with their king, queen and attendants. One looking-glass, eight feet by four feet eight inches, and two oval ones, ornamented with sconces; a beautiful cabinet, with Indian figures, &c. The ceiling is richly ornamented by Rose, with figures of Bacchus, Ariadne, Diana, Endymion, Venus,

Adonis, Cephalus, and Procris; the centre is said to be Colcas, a Roman officer, casting himself from his horse into the river Tiber.

STATE DRESSING ROOM.

Thirty feet two inches, by twenty-two feet three inches, nineteen feet five inches high, with a cove ceiling richly ornamented by Rose; the furniture green and gold, the room is hung with green damask, bordered with gold. An elegant chimney-piece of white marble, supported by fluted columns with Corinthian capitals; here are two elegant looking-glasses, and four beautiful pictures by Sir Joshua Reynolds. The Right Honourable the present Earl of Harewood, in a Spanish dress; Right Honourable the late Lady Harewood, in the character of Penseroso, with her infant, the eldest daughter, Frances; (the late Lady Frances Douglas.) The full-length portraits of the Countess of Harrington and Lady Worsley.

SALOON.

Thirty-six feet three inches, by twenty-four feet two inches, twenty-one feet one inch high; with two recesses, whose roofs are supported by composite Corinthian columns, painted, resembling siena marble, the furniture green and gold; here are the following paintings by Dall, dated 1773, viz. Harewood castle, Aisgarth Foss, Knaresbro' Castle, Richmond Castle, also two views of Plumpton Rocks, by Wm. Turner, Esq. R. A. over two highly-finished chimney-pieces of white marble, by Vangilder, are the sacrifices of Venus and Bacchus, in Bronze, by Collins.—A cove ceiling, richly ornamented, with Venus in a sea car, and Phæton in the chariot of the sun; two oval looking-glasses, under which are two elegant commodes, well filled with books, &c. From this room you walk out upon the fine portico, on the south front, which delights you with its beautiful home scenery, enriched by the sheet of water, a glimpse of the temple, and an immense plantation, extending itself as far as the eye can reach.

YELLOW DRAWING ROOM.

Thirty feet three inches, by twenty-two feet two inches, eighteen feet one inch high; the furniture yellow and silver; the room is hung with yellow damask, and bordered with silver. Here are four looking-glasses highly-finished, the cieling, from which is suspended a beautiful lamp, is richly ornamented in stucco, and the floor is covered with a rich carpet to correspond. This room has an elegant chimney-piece of white marble, embellished with the emblems of love, &c. and under one of the looking-glasses, is a rich side-table, most beautifully inlaid with musical ornaments, and the frame covered with silver. In one corner, is a marble bust of the late Mr. Pitt, by Fisher, placed on a wood column, painted in imitation of porphyry marble. Over the doors are portraits of the Right Honourable Edward, the late Lord Lascelles, by Hopner, and the Right Honourable Henry, the present Lord Viscount Lascelles, by Mr. Jackson.

WHITE DRAWING ROOM.

Thirty-eight feet nine inches, by 21 feet nine inches, seventeen feet four inches high ; the furniture white and gold, the room is hung with white damask, and bordered with gold. This room is as handsome as design and gilding can make it, the ceiling terminates in a cove, and most beautifully embellished with gilt ornaments, with pictures of Apollo, Juno, Bacchante, Venus, and Cupid ; likewise a stately chimney-piece of verde antique, ornamented with white marble, supported by two beautiful figures, and the fire-place embellished with Venus and Cupid in the centre. Here are five elegant looking-glasses, richly ornamented with gilt figures, &c. under two of which, are two magnificent side-boards, with marble slabs, richly inlaid with figures, &c. The frames are richly gilded, and underneath are two Cupids ; two full-length portraits, one of the Right Honourable the late Lord Harewood, by Sir Joshua Reynolds, and the other, is the Right Honourable the present Earl of Harewood, in his parliamentary robes, by Hopner.

GALLERY.

This room extends over the whole west end of the house, and is seventy-six feet six inches, by twenty-four feet three inches, twenty-one feet three inches high ; it is truly elegant, and presents such a show of magnificence and art, as eye hath seldom seen, and words cannot describe.— On one side of this room, are four most superb French plate looking-glasses, nine feet five inches, by seven feet six inches, and one of the same size over the fire-place, with two oval ones, ornamented with glass chandeliers; a most superb chimney-piece of white marble, supported by two elegant figures of nymphs; and ornamented with the triumph of Venus, by Vangilder, four elegant side-boards, with two slabs of marble each, by Fisher, the frames by Mr. Chippendale, of London. The pillars and pilasters are painted by Mr. Hutchinson, of London, in imitation of the verd antique marble, and admirably transcribed from a table in the same room. Over the seven windows, are some rich mock curtains, hanging in festoons, and apparently ready to let down at pleasure, they are formed of wood, carved and painted under the directions of Mr. Chippendale of London, in so masterly a manner as to deceive every beholder. Here are six beautiful tripods, carved and gilded; also in the four corners, are placed on pedestals, the following marble busts, Faustina, Homer, Caracalla, and Commodus. Over the two doors, are the portraits of the Right Honourable the Viscountess Lascelles, and the Right Honourable Lady Mary Ann York, by Hopner. The ceiling is of the palmyran taste, and the stucco work, by Rose, is esteemed the first of its kind in England. The paintings are admirably executed by Rebecca, and represent the seasons of the year, intermixed with the following figures from heathen Mythology. viz. the Judgment of Paris; Vulcan presenting a helmet to Jupiter, with his Cyclops making thunderbolts for him; Europa, who was carried away by Jupiter, in the shape of a bull through the sea to Crete; Jupiter and Juno, trying Venus for marrying Vulcan; Aurora, in her triumphal car; Mercury, holding Meduses' head cut off by the order of Minerva, to be fixed on her shield, and all that looked on were turned into stone; A sacrifice to Ceres, the goddes, of corn and flowers; Venus in her triumphal car, drawn by two doves, attended by the graces; Neptune, in his sea car, holding a trident in his hand; assembly of the gods and goddesses; a feast of Bacchus; Apollo and the nine muses; and many other fancy paintings, on the frames of the looking-glasses, &c.

DINING ROOM.

Thirty-eight feet eight inches, by nineteen feet ten inches, seventeen feet two inches high; with a large recess over the fire-place, which is of white marble, richly carved, and in the centre is a beautiful basket of fruit and flowers, are Venus and Cupid in stucco. In two elegant gilt frames against the wall, are the portraits of the late Right Honourable Wm. Pitt, and the late Right Honourable Spencer Perceval, the first by Hopner, and the latter by Sir Thomas Lawrence; two rich looking-glasses, under which are two elegant side-boards, richly inlaid; likewise two others under the fore-mentioned portraits. On the walls, are the following paintings by Zucchi: viz. the Four Seasons; a Grecian dance; binding of Bacchus with ivy bands; the Rape of Helena; a Festival of Bacchus.

MUSIC ROOM.

Thirty-six feet six inches, by thirty feet, nineteen feet two inches high; the furniture scarlet and gold. Here are the following magnificent paintings of ruins, &c. by Zucchi: St Mark's Place at Rome, with Trajan's Pillar, taken on a market-day; a View of Naples; the inside of the Pantheon at Rome; the Ruins of Dalmatia. Over an elegant ornamented chimney-piece of white marble, is a full-length portrait of the late Mrs. Hale, in the character of Euphrosyne, by Sir Joshua Reynolds. The ceiling is divided into compartments, by cornices elegantly carved; in the divisions, are the Judgment of Midas, Minerva and the nine muses; in the four corners, are Europe, Asia, Africa, and America, by Rebecca; the floor is covered with a beautiful carpet to correspond. Here are two elegant pier glasses, eight feet by four feet four inches, under which, are two richly inlaid tables; also a most beautiful and superb glass chandelier, with twelve burners, suspended from the ceiling.

CIRCULAR ROOM.

Twenty feet in diameter, the furniture blue and white; here is a pier glass so placed, that each single object reflects seven representations. The ceiling terminates in a dome, supported by sixteen pilasters, with Ionic capitals, and is richly ornamented, with an antique marriage; the rape of Proserpine; a Group of the Muses; Jupiter, Juno, and Neptune, petitioning a Roman emperor, by Milo, and four paintings of boys playing, by Zucchi.

BEST STAIR-CASE.

Thirty-three feet by seventeen feet, forty-eight feet high, six feet within the rails; an elegant glass lantern is suspended from the Ceiling; with a beautiful lamp in the inside, and six others for lamps occasionally, in the corners; some glass cases with curious birds stuffed. The walls are painted in imitation of sienna, and the columns are of porphyry marble, by Mr. Hutchinson, and decorated with the following paintings by Zucchi; Aurora in her car; the Birth of Venus; Triumph of Venus; the Triumph of Bacchus, and a South-East View of the House and Grounds, by Dall; dated 1773. The second landing is in one solid stone, eighteen feet by six feet. Before leaving the house, the stranger should notice the handsome and massy mahogany doors, there are 74 in number, after which I will conduct him to the

GARDENS AND PLEASURE GROUNDS

Which have long and deservedly been celebrated as the first in the north of England, they were partly laid out by Mr. Brown of Hampton Court, and a part of them by Mr. Sparrow, a part by Mr. White, and very great additions have been made of late years by Mr. James Webb, who has lived at Harewood House upwards of forty years, and was one of Mr. Brown's pupils. The gardens abound with every convenience for producing the finest fruits, flowers, and exotics. The pleasure grounds are truly elegant and extensive, and admirably planned; shrubs of every sort are seen to flourish luxuriantly, which are judiciously mixed. On leaving the stately mansion, to see those elegant gardens and grounds, the stranger is conducted first through the

c

FLOWER GARDEN,

Which is finely contrived, and neatly kept by Mr. Chapman, the gardener, who has lived at Harewood House as Gardener, nearly forty years. In this garden is one of the finest weeping ashes in the kingdom, and many others in different parts of the grounds. In the summer season, the green-house plants are brought up here, and placed against the end of the house; from hence, we cross the lawn, where we have a beautiful view of the south front of the house. Then we come to the

MASON'S HARBOUR.

A neat little stone building covered with Ivy, said to have taken its name from the masons sheltering here during the time the house was building. Proceeding from hence, down the walk, at a small distance are the

STABLES,

A magnificent building of the Tuscan order, begun April 1755, and finished about 1757. From hence, descending the hill to the fish-pond, look on the left, and at a small distance is seen the stone alcove.

Throughout this whole scence of variety, the improvements are adopted to follow the luxuriant fancy of nature, and humour her different propensities: you see her decked out and enriched, where necessity or propriety bespeak indulgence; in the simplicity of her own dress, where ornament would disguise her beautiful attire. A scene, best described in the following lines.

" The lake, the island, and the birds,
" A living landscape spread ; the feather'd fleet,
" Led by the mantling swans, at every creek
" Now touch'd, and now unmoor'd ; now on full sail,
" With pinions spread, and oary feet, they ply
" Their vagrant voyage ; and now, as if becalm'd,
" 'Tween shore and shore, at anchor seem to sleep.
" Around the shores, the fowls that fear the stream,
" At random rove : hither, hot Guinea sends
" Her gadding troop ; here, 'midst his speckled dames,
" The pigmy chanticleer, of Bantam, winds
" His clarion ; while, supreme, in glittering state,
" The peacock spreads his rainbow train, with eyes
" Of sapphire bright, irradiate each with gold.
" Meanwhile, from every spray, the ringdoves coo,
" The linnets warble, captive none, but 'lur'd
" By food, to haunt the umbrage: All the glade
" Is life, is music, is liberty, and love."

MASON'S GARDEN.

Now we either cross the beautiful piece of water in a boat to the garden, or walk a short distance round the head of it, where is a cover'd seat, from which you have a fine view of the water, hills, &c. At the head of this water, formerly stood a large corn-mill, but was pulled down in 1775. When Mr. Chapman's (the Gardener) house was built, the masons found a stone which came out of the ruins of this mill, and put it in the west wall, where it is now to be seen, with the following inscription on it. "This mill was rebuilt by John Boulter, Esq. 1706. And in the centre of the stable-yard, is a large mill-stone which came from the same place.

Proceeding onward, we cross a wooden bridge, the instant we get over, stepping about a yard to the right is seen a beautiful waterfall, of about fourteen feet ; after which we pass through a wood of very fine old oak, beech, &c. which goes by the name of Crow Wood, formerly a rookery.

Adjoining this wood, are the much-admired

gardens of about seven acres, divided into five parts by double brick walls, about fifteen feet high. We first begin in the green-house, which stands in the herb garden, and measures seventy-one feet in length, and seventeen feet and a half in width, and fifteen feet in height; designed by Mr. Chapman, from this place we proceed through two peach-houses, in the old garden, and then into two gardens called the new gardens, and return a small distance into the stove garden, where are the fig-house, a peach-house, two vineyards, conservatory, little pine-house, and the great pine-house, which excels all the other; measures one hundred feet in length, in width thirty feet, and in height fifteen feet; disigned by Mr. Chapman. Pines have been cut in this house nearly twelve pounds weight, and grapes nearly eight pounds the bunch. In this hot-house are two very fine granadillas, which seem perfectly at home, and enjoy as much health and vigour, as if they were in the island of Jamaica; the whole of the gardens are under the management of Mr. Chapman.*

Near half a mile from the house, are the menagerie, farm-yard, workshops for the different artizans, and a variety of other offices, forming altogether, an elegant little village.

From whence we proceed by the pleasure grounds, where a prospect of unrivalled beauty, the vale of Wharfe unfolds itself, placid, open, lovely, and luxuriant; combining the milder attributes of landscape, with an air of dignity and features of magnificence.

---

* In 1818, was cut in this garden, a melon, which weighed nearly twelve pounds.

From the rising of the walk, we perceive all at once, a fine north view of the house where the carriages and horses are in waiting on a Saturday for the company, during the Harrogate season, if they should find themselves fatigued, by following the walk, through the gateway to the house, but by following the pleasure ground, we soon come to a fine opening made for the purpose of a view of Alms-Cliff from the hall door, and from hence, is a most beautiful view of Wharfedale, and the hills forty miles distant, with the town of Otley, Farnley, the seat of Walter Fawkes, Esq. Bramhope, Arthington, with the Nunnery, the residence of Mrs. Lambe, Weardley Mount, Village, &c.

> Rich are the views that now before us rise,
> Where nature charms, and genius darts surprize:
> Group'd are the lordly domes that wide display
> The sprightly valley and the winding way.

Here the walk branches off in three directions, and meet in one again above the church; but we must stop here and see the

OCTAGON SEAT.

Which stands on a rising ground, and is fixed on a mount, it has one door, and two steps into it, and eight canvass blinds, to shut up quite close, or let down at pleasure.
The tourist may proceed either in the centre walk, or in the south walk, where is another curious seat facing the house, but I will recommend one of the north walks, where stands a beautiful

ROTUNDO.

There is not a piece of stone-work in the whole gardens or grounds, that makes a more beautiful figure, than this majestic edifice ; it is an airy building, with an elegant dome; here are two openings, one for a view of Alms-Cliff, and the other for a view of the Castle, likewise a part of Wharfedale. Just by is the ancient Parish Church, which we must call and see, in our way to the Castle and Village.

THE CHURCH.

This Church is situated about half a mile west of the village, and about four hundred yards north-east of Harewood House. It is a very ancient and venerable pile, surrounded by a thick grove of trees, whose close embowering shade, is a pleasing addition to the solemnity of the place : the west end is beautifully mantled with ivy, it is a vicarage, dedicated to the Holy Cross and by the old time, (Old Holy Rood) the inhabitants keep their annual feast, which is the first Sunday after Old Holy Rood.

It is said, that this Church was founded by William de Curci, in the 17th of Henry I. 1116. In the year 1793, when the Church was new roofed, was found, on the old beam, the following inscription, cut in ancient characters, which was made away with, by the workmen. The English of it was thus.

"We adore and praise thee, thou holy Jesus, because thou hast redeemed us by thy Holy Cross."—Dated 1116.

This Church belonged to the patronage of the

Lords of the manor, till the 4th of March, 1353. Sir John de Insula, Lord of Rugemont, Knt. obtained the apostolic letters, whereby he got it appropriated to the Prior and Convent of Bolton in Craven, to which monastery he granted the right of patronage thereof; in regard to his ancestors who had been benefactors to the same house.

And there was reserved out of the fruits thereof, to the archbishop and his successors, two marks per annum, and to the dean and chapter of York, one mark yearly, payable on Michaelmas day: also a competent portion for a perpetual Vicar therein, to be instituted at the presentation of the said Prior and Convent! the portion of whose vicarage shall consist in twenty-two marks* sterling, yearly, payable by the said Religious to the Vicar for the time being, on the Octaves of St. Martin, and on the Octaves of Pentecost. And as to all the extraordinary burdens of the same church, and the repairs and new building of the chancel, the Prior and Convent shall bear them; as oft as need requires: the Vicar only bearing ordinary burdens encumbent on the Church; and on the last of March, 1354, the Chapter of York confirmed this appropriation made under the Archbishop's seal, &c. yet it must be observed, that the Church of Harewood, was (by ordination of Walter Grey, Archbishop) to pay certain tithes out of it to the Chapel of St Mary and Holy Angels.†

Because it ever was a custom that no church should be consecrated till it was endowed, it may

---

* Thirteen shillings and four-pence each. † Burton's Monastican.

give lawful occasion to enquire and record, what revenues this Church of Harewood is endowed with, Anno Domini 1681, and the particulars are as follows, A good Vicarage House (which I found ruin'd, but left repaired) gardens, one croft, a cowgate in the castle park, a close in Bonegate, containing by estimation about two acres, the church-yard and surplice fees, and mortuarys, and the annual stipend of twenty-two marks,* to the truth of which, I with divers others, do subscribe our names.

*George Ogden, late Minister of Harewood.**
- In the body of the Church were formerly some very antique oak seats, the whole was common, and the assembly promiscuous. The present elegant pews were erected in the year 1798, in the choir were six very curious stalls, for the six priests, during the solemnity of high Mass, which was performed every day; they were all destroyed when the above pews were erected; at the same time were taken away the old altar rails, on which was carved the initials of the Earl of Strafford's name, the only memorial left of the Wentworth family, and new ones erected, with a new singing loft, and a pew on each side for the Earl of Harewood's servants.

The Advowson of Harewood, continued to Bolton Priory till the dissolution, when it seems again to have come to the Lords of the manor, and after the death of John Boulter, Esq. in 1738, alternately to the parishoners of Harewood, and the heirs of lady Elizabeth Hastings; the Rev. R. Hale is the present Vicar; its annual value is between four and five hundred pounds.

---

* Extract from the Register Book.

This Church cannot fail to attract the notice of the curious, a person attends every Saturday during the Harrogate season, to shew the company, when on their way to and from Harewood House; on other days application must be made to the clerk, in the village, for the key.

The windows of this Church, particularly the east window, was elegantly ornamented with a priest, in his proper habit, with many other effigies, and insignia of its various ancient Lords, but they were all destroyed by the working people, in the year 1793, and the windows new glazed with plain glass; the painted glass was not deposited in the store-room at Harewood House, as Dr. Whitaker relates in his History of Leeds, for the author of this small work has discoursed with some of the people that took part of it away, every body took what they liked, and since that time, their children have destroyed it all.

Here is a peal of three bells, but there has been more formerly, and a very good clock, the gift of the late Edwin, Lord Harewood, it came from Plumpton; also an elegant organ with nine stops, built by Mr. John Donaldson of York, it was the gift of the present Edward, Earl of Harewood, which will be seen by the following memorandum in front of the organ.

"This Organ was opened on Sunday July 15th, 1804; the Gift of the Right Honourable Lord Harewood. The Rev. Rd. Hale, Vicar, C. B. Brooke, Clerk, John White, Organist. July, 1804.

The roof of the Church is supported by two rows of strong octagan columns, with light Gothic arches.

In number and perfect preservation of the

tombs of its Lords, this Church probably sur-
passes every parish church in the county. In
the choir, are six altar tombs of white alabaster;
on each are placed fine whole-length figures of
some of the ancient owners of this manor, with
many other elegant monuments, grave stones,
&c. which will be better apprehended, by the
following plan of the Church.

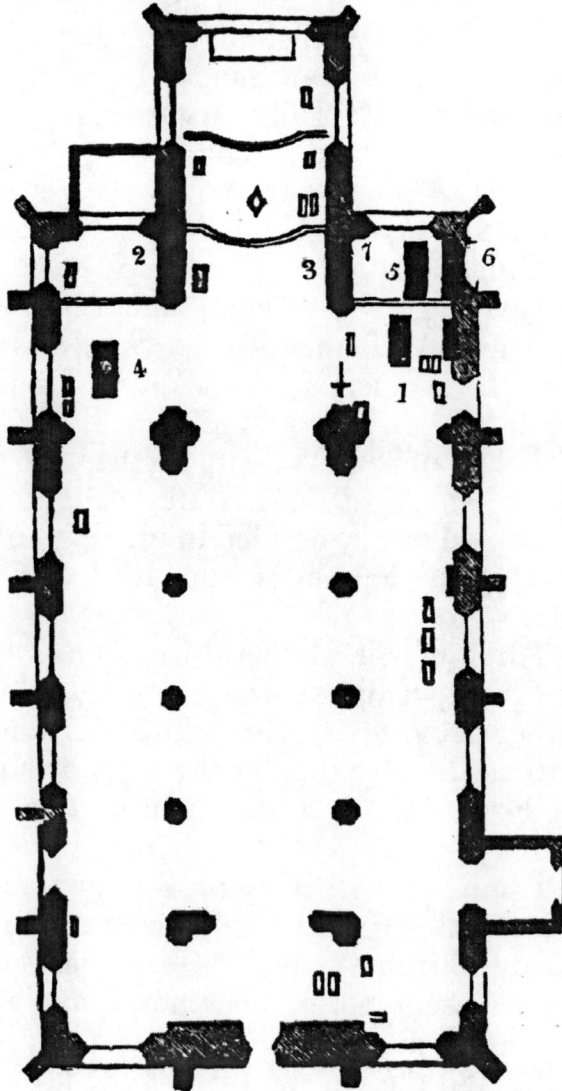

1. The tomb of Sir William Gascoigne, of Gawthorpe, Knt. Chief Justice of England; and Elizabeth his wife, daughter and co-heiress of Sir William Mowbray, of Kirklington, Knt.— He died the 17th of December, 1412. Round the verge of this tomb, on a brass fillet, (torn away in the civil wars) was the following inscription:

" Hic Jacet Willielmus Gascoigne, Nuper Capitalis Iusticar de Banco Henrici, Nuper Regis Angliæ; Et Eliza, uxor ejus qui quidem Willielmus, Obet die dominica 17th Madie Decembris, Anno domini 1412.

The English,—" Here lies Wm. Gascoigne, lately Chief Justice of the Bench of Henry the Fourth, King of Scotland, and Elizabeth his wife; which William died on Sunday the 17th Day of December, in the Year of our Lord, 1412.

2. Tomb of Sir William Ryther, of Ryther, Knight; and Sybil, his Wife, daughter of Sir William Aldburgh, he died in the reign of Henry VI:—On his helmet is the Ryther Crest, a dragon.

3. Tomb of Sir Richard Redman, of Harewood Castle, Knight; and his Lady, Elizabeth, the other daughter of Sir William Aldburgh of Harewood, he also died in the reign of Henry VI, —On his helmet is a horse's head, the Crest of this family.

4. Tomb of Sir Richard Redman, Knight; Grandson of Sir Richard, before-mentioned; and Lady Elizabeth, his Wife, daughter of Sir William Gascoigne, of Gawthorpe, Knight.

5. This Tomb, by the Arms, (Gules, a Saltier Argent; and the Crest, a Bull's Head) is said to

be a Neville, probably Sir John Neville, of Womersley, Knight, who died in 1482; and whose daughter and heiress, Joan married Sir William Gascoigne, Knight.—This Tomb has often been mistaken for the unfortunate Earl of Strafford's.—The Earl was interred in the family vault, in Wentworth Castle.

6. This Tomb is said to be that of Sir Richard Frank, and his Wife, of Alwoodly Hall, by some supposed to be a Thwaites and his wife,

7. The Monument of Sir Thomas Dennison, Knight, a Judge in the King's Bench, and under a well-cut Bust of the Judge, is an inscription, said to have been written by William, Earl of Mansfield, who was his particular friend.

To the Memory of
Sir Thomas Dennison, Knt.
This Monument was erected
By his afflicted Widow.
He was an affectionate Husband, a generous Relation,
A sincere friend, a good Citizen,
An Honest Man.
Skill'd in all the Learning of the Common Law,
He raised himself to great Eminence
In his Profession;
And shew'd by his Practice,
That a thorough Knowledge of legal Art and form
Is not litigious, nor an instrument of Chicane,
But the plainest, easiest, and shortest way,
To the End of Strife.
For the Sake of the Public,
He was pressed, and at last prevail'd upon,
To accept the Office of a Judge,
In the Court of King's Bench.
He discharg'd the important Trust
Of that High Office,
With unsuspected Integrity and uncommon Ability.
The Clearness of his Understanding,
And the natural Probity of his Heart,
Led him immediately to Truth, Equity, and Justice.
The Precision and Extent of his legal Knowledge,
Enabled him always to find the right Way,
Of doing what was right.

A zealous Friend to the Constitution
Of his Country,
He steadily adhered to the fundamental Principle,
Upon which it is built,
A religious Application of the inflexible Rule of Law,
To all Questions concerning the Power of the Crown,
And Privileges of the Subject.
He resign'd his Office February 14th, 1765,
Because from the Decay of his Health,
And Loss of Sight,
He found himself unable any longer to execute it.
He died September 8th. 1765, without Issue,
In the 67th Year of his Age.
He wish'd to be buried in his native Country,
And in this Church.
He lies here
Near the Lord Chief Justice Gascoigne,
Who by a resolute, and judicious Execution of Authority,
Supported Law and Government, in a Manner,
Which has perpetuated his Name,
And made him an Example famous to Posterity.

8. This Monument is on the South Wall, to the Memory of Dame Ann Dennison,* with the following Inscription.

In the same Vault with those of
Her late Husband,
Sir Thomas Dennison, Knt.
And agreeable to her Will
Are deposited the Remains of
Dame Ann Dennison,
Daughter of Robert Smithson, Esq.
She departed this Life
The 1st of July, 1785,
In the 72d Year of her Age.

---

* It appears from a codicil to Dame Ann Dennison's will, (dated 21st September 1782) that she left the interest of £20. in the 3 per cent consols, (now amounting to £40. in the 3 per cent consols) for beautifying and keeping in repair, the above Monuments of Sir Thomas Dennison, and that of her own Dame Ann Dennison; and if any surplus annually remains after deducting the expences, to distribute the same amongst such poor person or persons of the same Parish, as the Trustees for the time-being, shall think proper.

9. In Memory of Fairfax Fearnley, who died October 29th, 1791.

10. The Family Vault of the Earl of Harewood, which was made in the Year 1795.

11. In Memory of Mr. Wm. Lodge, who died in the Year 1689, aged 40 Years.

12. In Memory of John Hepworth, Vicar, he died in 1701, aged 72 Years.

13. In Memory of Edmund Boulter, who died in 1736, aged 57 Years.

14. On two Brass Plates is the following Inscription, in Memory of the Rev. Chr. Jackson, A. B. Vicar of this Church 28 Years, he died 27th December, 1792, aged 70 Years. Also Elizabeth Jackson, Wife of the above Rev. C. Jackson, She died 2nd of August, Aged 73 Years.

15. In Memory of Robert Knight, Vicar, who died in 1747, aged 68 Years.

16. A Cross cut in the Flag Stone, in Memory of the Dedication of the Church.

17. To the Memory of John Anley, Gent. he died 3d of April, Anno Domini 1681.

18. In Memory of Mr. John Hargrave, he died in 1687.

19. Here lies deposited the Remains of Henry Waugh of Leeds, who departed this Life, the 11th of June, 1790, aged 73 Years. Also, two Children of Thomas and Ann Harrison, of Stubhouse, and Grandchildren to the above Henry Waugh.

20. On a brass Plate let into the Flag, is an Inscription to the Memory of Samuel Popplewell, and Sarah his Wife, he died in September 1780, she died in September 1779. Under the Children's Seats, are the Remains of Mr. Samuel Popplewell, Steward, (upwards of 30 Years) to

the late Lord, and the present Earl of Harewood, Son of the aforesaid Mr. Samuel and Sarah Popplewell, he died the 19th of July, 1811; aged 70 Years. Also Charlotte, the Daughter of Samuel and Ann Popplewell.

This Inscription was on a Stone where the late Mr. Samuel Popplewell was buried.

" Here lies the Rev. John Westerman, who died September 15th, 1771, aged 27 Years. During the short space of Life, he discharged the sacred duties of his profession with the sincerest diligence, and died lamented by all his Friends.—RESURGAM.

21. Under the Sunday Scholars Seat, cut in the Flag, is the following Inscription.

Here lieth interred the Body of
Charles Bateman of Harewood, who
departed this Life,
the 27th Day of August, Anno 1719,
In the 37th Year
Of his Age.

22. Here was the ancient Family Vault of the Mallorys of Dunkeswick, it is said, this Stone with many others, was defaced by the Masons when the Church was new flagged—Matthew Mallory, who died in 1619, was interred here.

23. Here lies the Remains of William Walker, late House Steward to the present Earl of Harewood, was in his Lordship's service 47 Years; he died October 1st, 1809. aged 70 Years.

24. The Remains of the Rev. William Cheldry: Vicar of Harewood, who died in the Year 1722.—This Stone is lost.

24. In Memory of Miss Grace, Daughter of the late Dr. Davison, who died February 5th, 1806.

Here also tradition States, was the Family Vault of the De Curcies, the founders of this Church; from the grave-stone which now lays in the church-yard, but which it appears has been inlaid with a Brass Fillet, and three Brass Plates, on two of which, were engraved, the figures of himself and his lady, and over their heads on the other plate, the arms of the Family.

Robert Glover, Esq. (Somerset Herald) made a visitation of the County of York, in 1585, as deputy to William Norroy, King of Arms, he surveyed Harewood Church, and noted all he then saw, which remains beautifully drawn in a manuscript, preserved in the Herald's College; and several antique tombs yet remaining; he mentions three other tombs not now to be found, with the following Inscriptions.

1st. " Orate pro anima Johis Thawits, Legis periti, ac Justicearii pacis in Com. Ebor. Ann. 66, qui obit 1469, et Isabella uxoris ejus, filia Willmy Ryther, Militis, que obit Ao Dni."

" Pray ye for the soul of John Thawits, Lawyer and Justice of the Peace, in the County of York, aged 66; who died in 1469, and Isabella his wife, Daughter of William Ryther, Knight, who died in the Year of our Lord,"........

2nd. Orate Pro Animabeie......Gascoigne, at Elizabeth et Johana Oxoram Suarum."

" Pray ye for the souls of ...... Gascoigne, and Elizabeth and Joan his wives.

3rd. " Orate Pro Alfredo Monston, et Eliza-uxoris ejus."

" Pray ye for Alfred Monston, and Elizabeth his wife."

Benefactions over the South Door.

The interest of £20 left by Michael Hawke, of Harewood, single man, in the year of our Lord, 1615.

The interest of £20 left by Robert Frank, Esq. of Alwoodley in the year of our Lord 1619.

The interest of £20 left by Stephen Harrison, of Stubhouse, in the year of our Lord 1620.

The interest of £5 left by Bridget Mallorie, in the year of our Lord 1622.

The interest of £5 left by James Burnley, of Burdenhead, in the year of our Lord 1636.

The interest of £5. donors name not known.

The above sums are all left for the use of the poor of the parish of Harewood.

To the poor of the township of Harewood, the interest of £10 left by Charles Bateman, of Harewood, in the year of our Lord 1719.

To the poor of the Township of Weeton, one close of ground called Wescho-hill Close, lying at Wescho-hill: left by William Wade, in the year of Lord 1722, lets at £5 per Ann. to the poor of the township of Weeton and Dunkeswick, the sum of 20s, to be paid yearly out of the estate of Mr. Robert Midgeley, lying at Weeton.

To the poor of the township of Eastkeswick, one moiety of certain lands and tenements lying at Clifford and Eastkeswick, the whole now let at £12. 5s. per Ann. left by Richard Dawson of Collingham, in the year of our Lord 1608.

Benefactions over the North Door.

To the poor of the parish of Harewood, two closes of ground, called Fox-glove-close, and Strake-foot-ing, lying at Weeton, left by Anthony Sawdrie, parish clerk, in the year of our Lord 1631. Also an allotment for the same, situated at Huby; the yearly rent to be used for putting out a boy or girl, apprentice yearly within the parish of

Harewood, viz. first year to Harewood, second year to Wike, Wigton, Alwoodley or, Weardley, third year to Eastkeswick, Dunkeswick or, Weeton, so that it goes to Harewood every third year, viz. first to Harewood, second to Wike, third to Eastkeswick, fourth to Harewood, fifth to Wigton, sixth to Dunkeswick, seventh to Harewood, eighth to Alwoodley, ninth to Weeton, tenth to Harewood, eleventh to Weardley.—None to have benefit, but such as are born in Wedlock, whose parents are inhabitants within the parish of Harewood. Within the space of 10 years, in defect of a boy or girl in any of the said places, the money to be laid out in grey cloth, and given to the poorest person there.

A house and garth at Huby: left by Thomas Harrison of Stubhouse, which with the lands before-mentioned, are now let for £9. 7s. 9d. a year.

Three acres of meadow ground lying in Eastkeswick fitts, left by James Flesher, merchant, of London, in the year of our Lord 1625, and now exchanged for seven acres or nearly, of land lying in the township of Eastkeswick, known by the name of Barnesleys land, which is now let at £5 per year, to the use of the poor of this parish.*

The Benefaction Boards painted 1799.

The church-yard formerly extended a great way further south and west, than what it does at present. We are told by tradition, that the school was on the south of the church-yard, and many other buildings where the officiating priest resided, to teach in the school, and perform daily mass in the church.

One William Fentiman, a taylor, of Harewood, who died not many years since, a very old man, remembered seeing the old ruins of the school and other buildings, about fifty yards south of the church.

---

* The cottage, garth, an allotment, and other lands at Huby, measuring five acres three roods and thirty perches, are now let for £10. 12s. 6d. per year, (viz.) £2. 12s. 6d. for the cottage, and £8 for the clerk's closes as above.

The land belonging to the poor of the parish of Harewood, lying in the township of Eastkeswick, containing nearly seven acres, is now let at the yearly rent of £6. 6s.

In the year 1791, in making the sunk fence for the pleasure ground, on the east side of the church-yard, were found many urns, filled with ashes and bones, painted various colours, likewise some stones with the cross and various other figures cut on them, part of them were in the possession of the late Mr. John Wood, of Harewood, who had a great taste for antiquity, and was an eye witness to most of the late alterations at the church, and about it, from him the author got a great deal of information; this person was in possession of some of the painted glass out of the east window, (so much talked of by the antiquarians,) who preserved it with the urns, &c. but by degrees they were dispersed and lost.

There is no doubt but here was a very large burying ground before this church was built, for in making some vaults, were seen some very large thigh, and other bones belonging to the human body, quite under the foundation of the church,

Rectors.

Robt. de Clepstone,	-	1275
Wm. Burnell,	- -	1280
John Burnell,	- -	1281
Wm. fil. Wm. Burnell,	-	1291
Humphry de Bellemonte,	-	1299
Roger de Ledes,	- -	1309
Humphry de Bello Campo,		1310
John de Welleton,	- -	1321
William de Popilton,	-	1345
Hugo Spotkyng.	- -	1350

This list was given to the Author, by Mr. Hargrove, of Knaresbro'.

Extracted from Torre's Archdeaconry of York---Page 172.
Harwood Ch.

A close Catalogue of the Vicars of Harwood.

Temp Instit	Vicarii Eccle.	Patroni.	Vacat.
		Pr'et Contus de Bolton.	
1354	Fr. Laur. de Wath Cangus domus de Bolton	iidem	p' resig.
1354	Fr. Tho. de Manyngham Cancus domus de Bolton	iidem	p' resig.
1354	Fr. Will. Basset Cancus Mon. de Bolton	iidem	p' mort.
1368	Fr. Tho. Kiddall Cancus do Bolton	iidem	p' resig.
1362	Fr. Laur. de Wath, Pbr.	iidem	p' mort.
1369	Fr. Will. Harwood Cancus Mon. de Bolton	iidem	
	Fr. Joh. de Langton Cancus	iidem	p' mort.
1406	Fr. Joh. Burton Cancus domus de Bolton	iidem	p' mort.
1428	Fr. Joh. Gargrave, Pbr. Cancus de Bolton	iidem	p' resig.
1431	Fr. Robt. Morland Cancus Reg. de Bolton	iidem	
1444	Fr. Robt. Morland	iidem	p' mort.
1462	Fr. Joh. York Cancus Reg. Prioratus de Bolton	iidem	p' mort.
1490	Fr. Joh. Greneacre, Pbr.	iidem	p' mort.
1517	Fr. Percivall Otteley vel Walker Cancus de Bolton	iidem	p' mort.
1566	Rich. Lamb, Cl.	Thomas Fairfax ar.	p' mort.
1570	Geor. Howes, Cl. vel Lewss	iidem	
1582	Lanc. Barwyck, Cl. B. A.	Thomas Fairfax mil.	p' resig.
1614	Math. Garfurth, Cl.	iidem	p' mort.
	No Vicar instituted from the Restoration till 1699.—John Hepworth.	By the King	By lapse.
1704	Wm Chedry	By the Abp. of York	By lapse.
1734	Robert Knight, A. M.	John Boulter, Esq.	
1747	Robert Hargreaves	Boulter Thomlinson	
1751	Richard Bainbrigg, B. A.	Lady Hastings' Trustees	
1764	Christopher Jackson, B. A.	Boulter Thomlinson	
1795	John Tattersall, A. M.	G. H. Wheeler	
1801	Richard Hale, A. M.	The Earl of Harewood	

After viewing the Church, we return to the pleasure grounds, and take a pleasant walk through the plantations, which brings us to the Castle, but we must first notice in our way, the walk that goes under the church-road, and rises into the main-walk again, just by a singular recess, called the

LING HARBOUR,

This rural retreat is built on the roots of trees, &c. and covered with ling, the floor is beautifully pebbled, next we come to the

ROCK ARCH,

Which is contrived with all imaginable art, by Mr. Webb, under the directions of Edward, the late Lord Lascelles. The road under it, and the church-road, leads out of the south, into the north park, through some very large rocks, (lately a stone quarry) where the surrounding country presents at once a picture full of the beautiful and grand.

THE CASTLE.

This beautiful ruin is nearly all covered with ivy, and situated on the steep slope of a hill rising southward, on the north side of the village, or what is commonly called Bondgate,*

---

* Bondgate probably took its name from the bond-servants that antiently lived there, belonging to the owners of the Castle.

and about eighty yards from the Harrogate road,
which road winds gradually down the hill towards
the vale of Wharf,* whose beautiful mazes
may be traced to a considerable distance, which
gives a softness and beauty to the scene; the
eye wanders with infinite delight across a beautiful extent of country, twenty miles distant
beyond York. On the other hand are prospects
of unrivalled beauty, the vale itself opens to view
the distant hills in Craven, the town of Otley,
and Otley Chiven; Farnley, the beautiful seat
of Walter Fawkes, Esq. Pool, Bramhope, the
seat of William Rhodes, Esq. Arthington Hall,
and Nunnery, Alms-cliff, Rigton, Dunkeswick,
and Kirkby-overblow, the residence of the Rev.
Dr. Marsham, &c. causing an endless variety of
picturesque beauties.

The extent of this Castle, when entire, must
have been very considerable; for, we now observe
a great quantity of ground, around the remaining
building, covered with half-buried walls, and
fragments of ruins.

Dr. Story was at Harewood in 1790, he made
mention of this Castle, not doubting but it had
been a place of great note, and pointed out many
places which had been adjoining, but now in
ruins and buried in the grass.

What remains of this castle, appears to have
been chiefly built by Robert de Lisle, in the time of
Edward I, and to have been completed by Sir
William de Aldburgh, in the reign of Edward
III, about the year 1327.

* This road was made about the year 1799, greatly to
the credit of the present Edward, the first Earl of Harewood, being of great utility to the public at large.

In the walls are marks of a high ridged roof having been let in over the state apartments, but beneath the high parapet wall, so as to leave room for a platform on each side, upon the leads above, secured by the parapet, which might be for the purpose of placing warlike engines.

The grand portal is on the east side, and is just high enough for a man to enter on horseback; this entrance was defended by a large portcullis, the groove of which, is yet very evident.

On the front of this portal, inside of the castle, are three shields of arms, that in the centre, is an orle for Baliol, on each side is a lion rampant, the arms of Sir William de Aldburgh; on the outside is an orle on one side, and a lion rampant on the other, with the following motto, in Saxo-Monastic characters.

Vat Sal be Sal.

Over this gateway was a chamber called the chapel; in the freeze round it, are twelve coats of arms cut in the stone. But the armorial bearings, with the quarterings, that were formerly in the castle, castle-chapel, and parish church of Harewood, are as follows: 1. Redman and Daincourt, 2. Huddleston, 3. Aldbrough, 4. Baliol, 5. Aldbrough, 6. Ryther, 7. Sutton, 8. Aldbrough, 9. Baliol, 10. Baliol, 11. Aldbrough, 12. Thwenge, 13. no name, 14. Aldbrough and Sutton, 15. Constable, 16. Ross, 17. Vipount, 18. Galloway, 19. Redman, and Aldbrough, 20. Ryther, his quarterings, 21. Thwayts, and Ryther, 22. Gascoigne and Mowbray, 23. Gascoigne and Pickering, 24. Maaston, 25. Lord

Lisle, 26. Stapleton, 27. Redman and Aldbrough, 28. Redman, 29. Redman and Stapleton, 30. Redman, 91. Windsore, 32. Redman, 33. Goscoigne, &c. 34. Manston, 35. Manston and Nevill, 36. Franke and Ellis, 37. Gascoigne and Heaton, 38. Thwayts, 39. Thwayts, 40. Gascoigne and Clarrel, 41. Thwayts, 42. Gascoigne and Mowbray, 43. Gascoigne, &c. 44. Franke, 45. Nevill.—*Dr. Whitaker.*

There appears to have been two or three large rooms on the ground floor, divided by strong partition walls. The north side, said to be the kitchen and scullery, under which, was the cellar. In the north-west corner was the draw-well, for supplying the castle with water, which was cleaned out in 1771, to the depth of eighteen feet, but found to be of no use, it was filled up again with rubbish. In the centre, and in a line with the chapel, (where in 1813 was some ash-trees planted) is said to have been the court room,* under which, was the dungeon. On the south side, was the hall, state apartments, &c. Entering the west doorway, of seven feet wide, into the great room, on the left-hand is a magnificent recess, which has much puzzled the antiquarians, it seems to have been built with the wall ; it has been repeatedly affirmed to be the tomb for the remains of the founder of the castle, but Dr. Whitaker says, " Who ever dreamed in those days of being interred in unconsecrated earth. The original slab has been

---

* It appears that the episcopal court exercised the power of executions, and there is now a place called Gallow-hill, alias Gallows-hill, in the vicinity of Harewood.

removed, and instead of a stone coffin, nothing appears but a mass of solid grout-work, while, instead of kneeling figures of priests and children, beneath appears on a sort of frieze, a light and elegant enrichment of vine-leaves and grapes. From this last circumstance, combined with its situation near the head of the high table, I am persuaded that it was no other than an ancient side-boad."

This castle, from its present ruins, appears to have been in figure a parallelogram, having its sides in the direction of the cardinal points of the compass. It has two square towers on its south-east and south-west angles, the first considerably the largest, they both contained four stories one above the other; the places for the floors are yet to be discerned, each of which had a fire-place and a good light.

"Where are the chiefs of old: Where are our kings of mighty name? The fields of their battles are silent. Scarce their mossy tombs remain: We shall also be forgot. This lofty house shall fall: Our sons shall not behold the ruins in the grass. They shall ask of the aged, where stood the walls of our fathers?"—*Ossian.*

Mr. Camden says, Harewood castle suffered in the civil wars; most likely it might, but it is said, that Sir John Cutler, a penurious man, who resided at Gawthorpe-hall, reduced a great part of it to ruin, for the sake of the stone and timber, for building farm-houses, barns, walls, &c. There is no doubt of it, for there is now (1819) one of the houses standing in Bondgate, inhabited by Mr. James Hummerstone, with the following inscription over the west-door, dated 1678. It is the only antient cottage in the village.

D

16 I·C 78

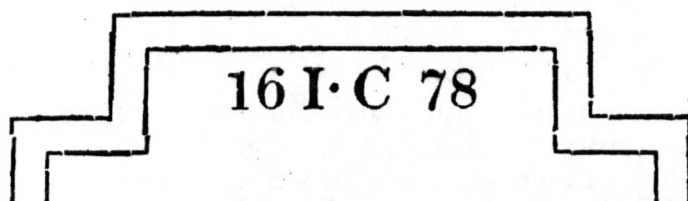

That benevolent gentleman, John Boulter, Esq. of Gawthorpe Hall, made an attempt to separate the stone for the use of building walls and farm-houses; but time had so compacted the cement, that the workmen soon desisted, finding they could procure materials from the quarry, at a much easier rate.*

On the west of this castle, are two very fine springs of water, one of which is called the Pigeon-well, which rises first out of the side of the hill, in the pleasure ground, and is conducted to a stone trough, by the road side, leading to Harrogate. The other is farther west, goes by the name of the Vicar-well, which it is said, took its name from rising in the friars close, in Bondgate, now enclosed in the park. This well is of great utility to the inhabitants, it is on the outside of the pleasure grounds, in the north park, and a long subterraneous passage under a arch, made for the purpose. " A spring of water rises in Lord Harewood's Park in Yorkshire, of remarkable purity. Its situation is at the southern extremity of the park, between three and four hundred yards westward of the turnpike road from Leeds to Harrogate. The water is scarcely affected by any tests but Nitrate of Silver, and

---

* When the Castle of Harewood was building, the master masons and carpenters' wages were only two-pence per day, but Wheat was then about four shillings per quarter, Oats and Barley ten-pence per quarter, a fat ox six shillings and eight-pence, a fat sheep sixpence, a fat pig one shilling, a fat goose two-pence.

Oxalate of Ammonia : six pints of it contain but thirty-three grains of dry salts, and from repeated analysis of that quantity, the following is the proportion of substances in a single pint."*

The pint contains	- - 0,55 of a grain, namely,
Muriate of Soda,	- - 0,325
Sulphate of Soda.	- - 0,151
Sulphate of Lime,	- - 0,066
Sul, Magnesia, trace of	———
	0,542

About half a mile west of the castle, and in the centre of a wood, which goes by the name of West-end-wood, was an open space, of about an acre; called Chasne-plain, which was kept cleared of trees, from a very remote period, but is now planted.

It has been said that this was the place where about the year 963, Earl Athelwold fell a sacrifice to the resentment of his royal master, king Edgar, seduced by the fascinating charms of the fair Elfrida, he forgot his duty to his prince, his benefactor, and his friend.

Higden in his Polichronicon, page 269, which ends about the year 1342, says,

" The Kynge had the Erle with hym, for to hunt in the Wode of Werwelley, † that now is called Hoore-Wode, ‡ there the kynge smate him through with a shafte."

The castle was taken into the new pleasure grounds, in the year 1813, and soon after, the castle-garden, where the cross walks were very plain to be seen, were planted, likewise the high bank that goes around it. At the same time, as the workmen were digging near the old ruin, they discovered some old broken sword blades, and pieces of spurs, which at that time, it ap-

* Journal of Science and the Arts, No. xi. p. 171.
† May not this be our Weardley. ‡ Now Harewood.

pears, they wore iron over the insteps instead of leather; many coins and other curiosities have been found at different times.

The present owner has made it emerge, with a consequence and lustre, that would do honour to any age and country, and it is still yearly rising in splendour.

I shall now decline mentioning several other seats and ornaments, with which these spacious gardens and grounds are embellished, only with this observation: a man of taste may enjoy himself in these beautiful walks, and may feel his mind expanded, his notions enlarged, and his heart better disposed, either for a religious thought, or a benevolent action. A taste for these exalted pleasures, contributes toward making him a better man, besides there is another great advantage in wealth, laid out in this elegant manner, which is this: the money spent in the neighbourhood, and the number of labouring poor, that are employed.

What a gratification ought this to be to so many fellow-creatures; such productions of art may be considered as a very great advantage to every neighbourhood, that enjoys the blessing of being placed near them.

It is impossible for a traveller, who has only a few hours to spare, to run through so great a variety of beauties, and not to let something escape his curiosity, or to remember exactly all he has seen, but by the help of drawing, he may carry a great deal more away with him, than by memory.

Having now gone round and given a faint description of this unparalleled chain of artificial and natural beauty; I may say with the poet,

" Here order in variety you see,
" Where all things differ, yet where all agree:

VISIT of the GRAND DUKE NICHOLAS,

OF RUSSIA,

On Tuesday December 10th, 1816.

His Imperial Highness arrived at Greaves's Hotel, in Leeds, on Monday evening, where the whole retinue remained during the night. Baron Nicolai. Sir Wm. Congreve, Generals Kutusoff and Woronzoff. Messrs. Clinkar and Mansell, Adjutant Perowsky, and Dr. Creighton, his Imperial Highness's Physician, were the chief attendants; the whole comprised about eighteen persons. On Tuesday morning, the young Prince and his suite, viewed the Cloth-Halls, and extensive Woollen Manufactory of Messrs. Wormald, Gott and Wormalds, one of our principal Flax-spinning-mills, and the great Iron-works of Messrs. Fenton, Murray, and Wood. About half-past three, they departed for Harewood-House. They arrived there about five, and were received at the grand entrance, by the noble Earl, and by Lord and Lady Lascelles :—the servants in their state liveries, lined the hall, and his Imperial Highness was ushered into the saloon, by the venerable Earl, and introduced to the numerous party of Nobility and Gentry assembled on the occasion, and afterwards conducted to his apartments. At seven o'clock, dinner was announced. The costly service of gold plate was in use, and the whole arrangements were of the most splendid and even princely description; but with entire re-

gard to true Old English Hospitality. A grand
Concert in the Gallery, under the direction of
the noble Earl's principal musician, with his
Lordship's band, the Church Choristers, &c.
followed; and the glee of the evening was main-
tained with uninterrupted eclat.—The following
morning, the Earl of Harewood conducted the
whole assemblage through the beautiful village
and pleasure grounds to the ancient Castle and
Church; at which his Imperial Highness expressed
his most unqualified approbation and delight; but
peculiarly so, on seeing every cottager busily en-
gaged in some work of usefulness or improvement
on his Lordship's estate. Not less than two
hundred, we hear, are regularly employed in this
manner; in fact, every labourer in the village,
wanting work, is instantly set upon it. This was
an establishment (as his Imperial Highness very
pointedly remarked) worthy an English Baron,
worthy every great man's imitation—such as
merited his own adoption at home. The young
Prince seems to be completely on the wing, active
in seeing every thing, and zealous for the adoption of English comforts.—So familiar, indeed,
was his Imperial Highness, with the numerous
labourers, that he took the spade from one of
them, and planted several young oaks, in the most
expert manner. After the gratifying promenade,
the party partook of an early dinner. With the
utmost regret, that the visit could not be longer
protracted, His Imperial Highness took his leave
on Wednesday afternoon, and proceeded to the
George Inn, York. On Thursday, his Imperial
Highness attended the morning service at the
Cathedral; and the travellers then proceeded to
Inverary, the seat of the Duke of Argyle.

It may be interesting to the reader, to be informed of the various possessors of Harewood, before it came into the hands of the present family.

TERRA REGIS.

iii *M.* In Hareuuode cu' berewicis h˙br TOR. SPROT 7 GRIM x. Car" ad g˙ld τr˙a ad iii Car. XL sol.

M. In Chesinc hb'TOR. v Car. bd g˙ld τ˙ra ad iii Caruc. xx sol.

When the general survey was made, in the time of William the Conqueror, Harewood was then a part of the king's demesne, and that therein, with its berwicks, were three manors, in which, Tor, Sprot, and Grim, probably three Saxon chieftains, were possessed of ten carucates of land, in Harewood, which were guildable, or paid to the taxes, land, was then valued at forty shillings.

In that reign, Harewood, together with the honour of Skipton in Craven, and other great estates in Yorkshire, came into possession of Robert de Romeli, by the Conqueror's gift, who had an only daughter, Cecily, who married to William de Meschines, Earl of Chester, he became Lord of the manor of Harewood.

This William de Meschines, and Cecily his wife, about the year 1120, founded the priory of Embsey in Craven, afterwards removed to Bolton. And after his death, the said Cecily, for the health of her soul, and of those of her sons, Ranulph and Matthew, gave to the Canon of Bolton, her Lordship of Kildwick, with the mill, and soke thereof; likewise that of Silsdon, and those of Harewood, with the sute thereto.

Cecily de Romeli, by her said husband, had two sons, before-mentioned, who both died without issue, and two daughters her co-heirs, Alice, who had the honour of Skipton, married, Fitz-Duncan, Earl of Mufrey, in Scotland, and nephew to Malcolm, king of that realm, Avice, married to William de Curci, steward of the household to Henry I, who had for her moiety, the manor of Harewood, with its dependencies, and other considerable estates.

This Avice, as well as her mother Cecily, and her sister Alice, in consideration, that they brought such great wealth to their husbands, retained their own family surname of Romeli, and from them, that large track of ground, adjoining their manor of Silsdon in Craven, called Romelies Moor, was denominated.

Avice de Romeli, also confirmed, to the Canons of Embsey, the mill of Harewood, which her mother had granted to them, as follows:

" Sciant omnes qui sunt, et qui venturi sunt, quod ego Avice, filia Cecilye de Romeli, concedo et presenti carta mea confirmo. Deo et beate Marie et Sancto Cothberto de Embsey, et Canonicis itm Deo servientibus, Molondina de Harewood, que mater Cecily dedit pdctis Canonicis in puram elmosinam, elemosinam, &c. pro salute anime mee, et pro salute animarum patris mei Willimi Meschini, et matris mee et successor meor his testib dno wllio filio Duncani, Alicia Sorore mea, witto de Curci, filio meo, et multis aliais."

" Know all, who are, and who shall be, that I, Avice, daughter of Cecily de Romeli, do grant, and by this my charter, do confirm, to God, and to the blessed Mary, and to Saint Cuthbert

of Embsey, and to the regular priests, who serve
God, at that place, the mills of Harewood, which
my mother Cecily gave to the aforesaid priests
in pure charity, &c. for the salvation of my own
soul, and for the salvation of the soul of my
father, William Meschins, and of my mother,
and of my successors : these being witnesses,
Lord William, son of Duncan, Alice my sister,
William de Curci my son, and many
others."

: To Avice de Romeli, succeeded William de
Curci, her son; who had an only daughter,
Alice, married Warine Fitzgerald, chamberlain
to king John, Lord (in her right) of this Manor;
and of Stoke-curry in Somersetshire, he had an
only daughter, Margery, his heiress, who married
first, Baldwin de Redvers, eldest son of William
de Redvers, Earl of Devonshire; which Baldwin
died in his father's life-time. Secondly, Fulk
de Brent; who from residing on his wife's
jointure lands, in the Isle of Wight, where the
family of Redvers had great possessions, was
denominated de Insula, or Lisle; and was
ancestor of Lord Lisle, of Rugemont.*

* Now goes by the name of Rugemont's-Scar, once the
seat of the ancient family of D'Insula; situated on the
northern bank of the river Wharf, which here, by a fine
and bold curve, forms a beautiful bay. The area, on
which the mansion stood, is about eighty yards by sixty,
moated round; the offices seem to have been at some distance, and the whole to have taken up near four acres,
encompassed by a rampart in some places, eighteen feet
broad. Sir John D'Insula, Lord of Rugemont, was living
in 1 53, In 1269, Robert Lord Lisle, of Rugemont, became
possessed of Harewood, on the death of his relation the
Countess of Lancaster, which will be seen hereafter.

This Margery de Redverrs, when residing at Harewood, granted to the nuns of Arthington, the tithe of her household expences there, as appears by the following deed.

"Ego Margery de Redvers in libera viduitate et legia potestate mea, confirmavi Deo et beate Marie et scis monialibus de Arthington, donationem quam Avice de Romeli eisdem contulit, viz. medeitatem terre de Healthwaite, &c.—et praterea totam decimam expense domusmee de manerio meo de Harewood, testes Ricardo de Mohrit, &c."

"I Margery de Redvers, in free widowhood, and by my own lawful power, have confirmed to God and to the blessed Mary, and to the holy nuns of Arthington, the donation, which Avice de Romeli conferred on them; namely, half of the land of Healthwaite, &c.—and besides the whole tythe of the expences of my house of my manor of Harewood, witness, Richard de Mohrit, &c."

To Margery de Redvers, succeeded Baldwin, Earl of Devon, her son, (during whose minority, the king committed the manor of Harewood, to Walter Gray, archbishop of York, Fines 9th of Henry III.) He had issue, a daughter, Isabel, his heiress, married to William de Fortibus, Earl of Albemarle.

In Kirby's inquest, made 13th Edward I, it was returned, that the Earl of Albemarle, held in Harewood, Carleton, Weardley, Wigton, Eastkeswick, and all that he held in the wapontake of Skyrack, of the king, for one knight's fee. and paid to the bailiff of Skyrac, twenty shillinggs for fine of the Wapontake.

William, Earl of Albemarle, rebelled against

Henry II, and manned his castle; but, was over-powered, and forced to submit. This William, Earl of Albemarle, by Isabel, his wife, had an only daughter, Aveline de Fortibus, their heiress; Countess of Albemarle, Devon, &c. the greatest fortune of her time, who married to Edmond Crouchback, Earl of Lancaster, son of king Henry III, who died without Issue, in the year 1269; upon the death of his Lady, much of their great estate was seized upon by the crown, particularly the Isle of Wight, the honours of Holderness, Skipton, &c. but the manor of Harewood, with its members, descended to her relation Robert Lord Lisle, of Rugemont, grandson of Margery de Redvers, her great grandmother by Fulk de Brent, her second husband, before-mentioned.

In the record called Nomina Villaru, made the 9th of Edward II, 1316, this Robert de Lisle, occurs as then Lord of the manor of Harewood, Keswick, and Kerby.

Robert Lord Lisle, was succeeded by John his son, who, in 1336, 10th of Edward III, that he might be the better enabled to serve the king in his wars, obtained from his father a grant of the manor of Harewood, then valued at four hundred marks per annum, to hold during his life.

In 1353, John Lord Lisle gave the church of Harewood to the prior and convent of Bolton, in Craven, in regard that his ancestors had been benefactors to that house; he died the 14th of October, in the 30th of Edward III, 1356, being succeeded by his son and heir, Robert.

Robert, Lord Lisle, who had an only daughter Elizabeth, married to Sir William de Aldburgh,

of Aldburgh, in Richmondshire, to whom and
Elizabeth his wife, Robert her Father, by the
command of king Edward III, in the 38th year
of his reign, for the sum of £1000, released all
his right to the manor of Harewood, with its
appurtenances.

" Fines Ao 38th Edward III.—Inter Willm.
de Aldburg, militem, et Elizabeth uxorem ejus
quærunt, et Robertum de Insula de Rubeo
Monte, defore de Manerio de Harewood, &c.
—Habend de eodem Willmo de Aldburgh et
Elizabeth et hered ipsius Willmi et præteria
idem Robertus concessit quod tertia pars pdti
manerii quam Matilda quæ fuit uxor Johis de
Insula de rubeo monte tenuit in dotem de
hereditate prædicte Roberti die quo hæc concordia facta fuit, rem precidicto Willo et Elizabeth
et heredbus ipsius Willmi, &c. et pro hac
recognitione, deditione, consessione, fine et
concordia, iidem Willus et Elizabeth dederunt
prædicto Roberto, mille libras sterlingorum et
hæc concordia facta fuit per præcepta ipsius
dni Regis."—

" Issues in the 38th year of Edward III,
between William de Aldburgh, knight, and
Elizabeth his wife, plaintiffs, and Rober Lisle
of Rugemont, who keepeth the proper heir out
of his right by force, concerning the manor of
Harewood, &c. to be held of the same William
de Aldburg, and Elizabeth, and the heirs of this
William; and moreover the same Robert hath
granted that the third part of the aforesaid
manor, which Matilda, who was wife of John
Lisle of Rugemont, held in dower of the inhe-
ritance of the aforesaid Robert, on the day in
which this agreement was made, should be held

by the aforesaid William and Elizabeth, and the heirs of the same William, and for this acknowledgment, restoration, concession, issue, and agreement, the said William and Elizabeth have given the aforesaid Robert a thousand pounds sterling, and this agreement was made by the commands of our lord the king.

Sir William de Aldburgh having thus obtained the manor of Harewood, seems to have made it his chief residence, and no doubt there was a castle here, in very early times, (Mr. Camden, giving an account of one here, prior to the reign of king John) this Sir William had two daughters, his co-heiresses; Elizabeth, married first to Sir Brian Stapleton, of Carlton; secondly, to Sir Richard Redman, of Redman, and Levens, in Westmorland, knight; and Sybil, to Sir William Ryther, of Ryther, knight; between whom, all his estate were divided.

In Hillary term, 17th of Richard II, 1393, a fine was levied, by Elizabeth, late wife of Sir Brian Stapleton, jun. and Sir William de Ryther, and Sybil his wife, daughters and co-heiresses of Sir William de Aldburgh, knight, deceased, of the manors of Harewood, Lofthouse, Stockhouse, Huby, Weeton, Rigton in the forest, Eastkeswick, Dunkeswick, Healthwaite, Horsforth, Yeadon, Weardley, Stockton, and Carlton, which were parcel of the manor of Harewood.

The husbands of both these ladies, died in the reign of Henry VI, and buried in Harewood church, under tombs, with the effigies of themselves, and their ladies, under the arches, on each side of the choir, Redman on the north, and Ryther on the south; as appears by the crests, under their respective heads.

The estates thus descending to co-heiresses, each family held them, in undivided moieties; but, the Redmans seem to have made the castle their principal residence, till the reign of Queen Elizabeth, in whose 21st year, 1578, both these families disposed of their property here.

The ancient family of Gascoigne, of Gawthorpe, * appears to have been the next owners of Harewood.

William Gascoigne, knight, obtained a licence, to inclose two parks here; the first, to contain two hundred and forty acres of land, in Gawthorpe, Weardley, and Harewood; the second, to contain seventeen hundred acres, in Henhouse,† Lofthouse, Weardley, Harewood, and Wike.

It is said in Magna Britannia, that Gawthorpe was a village in Harewood parish, midway between Leeds and Knaresborough, famous only for that ancient, virtuous, and warlike family of the Gascoigns, two of which, both knights, and named William, were high sheriffs of this county, the one 20th Hen. VI, and the other 1st Hen. VII. But before either of these, there was a knight of this family, born in this place, named also Sir William Gascoign, far more famous than they. He was bred up in our municipal laws in the inner temple, London, and grew so eminent for his skill and knowledge in them, that he was made chief justice of the king's

---

- * Dr. Whitaker says, Gawthorpe itself gave name, and abode to a family seated there, as early as the origin of local surnames.

† Now goes by the name of Hencroft, about a quarter of mile east of the Castle, where it is said, was the poultry-yard, belonging to the Castle.

bench, by king Hen. IV. Reg. 11, and held that place till 14 Hen. IV. demeaning himself all that time with admirable integrity and courage, as this example will shew.

It chanced that a servant of prince Henry, (afterwards king Henry V.) was arraigned before this judge for felony, and the prince being zealous to deliver him out of the hand of justice, went on to the bench in such a fury, that the beholders thought he would have stricken the judge, and attempted to take his servant from the bar. But this judge knowing whose person he represented, sat unconcerned, and knowing the prince's attempt illegal, committed the prince to the king's bench, there to remain a prisoner, till the king his father's pleasure was known. This action was soon represented to the king, with no good will to the judge; but it proved for his advantage; for when the king heard what his judge had done, he said, he thanked God for his infinite goodness, that he had at once given him a judge who dared to administer justice, and a son that could submit to it. Yea the prince himself, when he came to be king, reflecting upon this transaction, thus expressed himself in relation to that judge; I shall ever hold him worthy of his place and my favour, for that act of justice, and wish all my judges may have the like undaunted courage, to punish offenders, of what rank soever; and after him another Sir William Gascoigne, knight, served as knight of this shire, 13th Henry VI.

William Gascoigne, Esq. the last of this line, had an only daughter, Margaret, his heiress, married to Thomas Wentworth, of Wentworth Woodhouse, Esq. whose son, William, (father of Thomas, Earl of Strafford) was seized of this and several other manors in the neighbourhood. The manor of Gawthorpe, Harewood, Wike, Eastkeswick, Hetherick, (now Stank) Weardley, Weeton, Wescoe-hill, Burton-leanard, Thorp-arch, Lofthouse-head, Stubhouse, and lands in Tick-hill, Sea-croft, Awston, &c. Balne in Yorkshire, and Belton, and Awthorpe, in Lincolnshire.

The unfortunate Earl of Strafford, resided at Gawthorpe Hall, during the gathering of that storm, which, at length, proved so fatal to him. He was beheaded on Tower-hill, in the 16th of king Charles I, 1641, and his body was embalmed, and sent into Yorkshire to be buried in the family vault.—State Trials.

His son William, second Earl of Strafford, inherited all the said estates, but his father having contracted many debts, during the civil wars, the property which the Wentworths inherited from the Gascoignes, was sold to discharge them, and it was chiefly purchased by Sir John Lewis, bart. and Sir John Cutler, knight : who had married two sisters, daughters and co-heiresses of Sir Thomas Foot, knight; Lord Mayor of London, in 1649, and they had both acquired great wealth, Sir John Lewis, by trading to the East Indies, and Sir John Cutler, as a merchant in London, and by excessive penury, for which he has been celebrated, and his name handed to posterity, by Mr. Pope the poet, and the wits of the age.—He died in the year 1693.

Mr. Pope in his epistle (of George Villiers, Duke of Buckingham, to Sir John Cutler) to Lord Bathurst, are the following lines.

There, victor of his health, of fortune, friends,
And fame, this lord of useless thousands ends.
His Grace's fate sage Cutler could foresee,
And well (he thought) advis'd him, ' Live like me."
As well his Grace replied, ' Like you, Sir John!
' That I can do, when all I have is gone !
Resolve me, reason, which of these is worse,
Want with a full, or with an empty purse ?
Thy life more wretched, Cutler, was confessed,
Arise, and tell me, was thy death more blessed ?
Cutler saw tenants break, and houses fall,
For very want ; he could not build a wall.
His only daughter in a stranger's pow'r,
For very want ; hecould not pay a dow'r.
A few grey hairs his rev'rend temples crown'd,
Twas very want that sold them for two pound.
What ev'n deny'd a cordial at his end,
Banish'd the doctor, and expelled the friend ?
What but a want, which you perhaps think mad,
Yet numbers feel, the want of what he had !
Cutler and Brutus, dying, both exclaim,
" Virtue ! and wealth ! what are ye but a name !"

The late mansion, Gawthorpe Hall, which stood about three hundred and fifteen yards south of the present elegant mansion, (Harewood House) used to be occasionally visited by its then owner. (Sir John Cutler, from London.) His method was to bring with him only one man, or a lad, as his servant, and to have a single joint made ready, which after their first warm onset, it served them cold until the bones were picked, when a supply was brought to satisfy in the same way.

The distance of the mansion from Harewood, was under a mile, whence he hired a woman to make his bed, twice a week, and to perform on that day, the arrear-work of the intervals.

Sir John is the person whom Pope has eternised with his added pudding on festivals. Such a parsimony reminds us of the miser described on the French stage, who to save his pale ink, omitted to make a stop or dot. And we remember a fact, where a rich miser, on lending an egg to a neighbour, suggested to his servant to weigh it, lest he might not have as large a one in return.

The following lines are taken out of Mr. Maude's History of Wharfedale.

> Lo! distant Gawthorpe's renovated face,
> Gawthorpe, the brilliant object of our chace.
> Thither, by whim or thrift, was Cutler led
> To scanty viand, and his thrice-laid bed,
> Where spidered walls their meagre fate bemoan'd.
> Not so the present day, where copious smile
> All that the heart can wish or time beguile.
> Throng'd with the horn of plenty by her side,
> Unceasing sits, in dignifying pride,
> The festive nymph, with all her buxom train,
> Delicious guardians of the plain.

A noted oak was formerly shewn near the old hall, under which Sir John Cutler used to sit; when a person, said to be the famous Nevison, of whom mention is made of robbing in Kent in the morning, and appearing in the evening of the same day at York, on the bowling-green, conveyed on the same mare, (a circumstance which operated with the force of an alibi,) sallied from a neighbouring wood to levy contribution, but the knight suspecting the nature of the visit, made a forced march, and in a critical moment secured his retreat into the house. The panic, however, with which he was seized by this assault, induced him to quit his retirement, and ever after to take a lodging in the town of Harewood, to exempt him from any such future surprize.—It is said, he died in the year 1693, leaving his estate to his only daughter, Elizabeth, wife of John Robarts, Earl of Radnor; with remainder, in case of failure of issue, to his relation, John Boulter, Esq.* who on her death, (1697) accordingly inherited it; and, of the heirs of this gentleman, it was purchased by Henry Lascelles, Esq. in 1739.

Mr. Thorseby, in his History of Leeds, printed in 1715, says, the present lord of the town, who is John Boulter, Esq. a person very generous and charitable, hath been a considerable benefactor to the church and poor of his parish; for ever since he hath come to this estate, he hath allowed a considerable sum to the Vicar for preaching every Lord's day in the afternoon, and catechising the children; and another to a school-master in the town, to teach all poor children of the parish gratis, reading, writing, and arithmetic.— He likewise makes mention of an ancient camp at Stank.

The arms of Cutler, are Azure, three Dragon's Heads erased Or, and a Chief Argent.:—The arms of Boulter,—Argent upon a Cheveron Gules, three Dead Men's Skulls of the first.

---

* He died about the Year 1737.

Having finished the account of the village of Harewood, it may not be amiss to give some description of remarkable places in the neighbourhood, and a short account of that beautiful river, Wharf.

GAWTHORPE,

As I have noticed before, was the patrimonial residence of Chief Justice Gascoigne, and the favourite retreat of his illustrious descendant, Thomas Earl of Strafford. They who enjoy, or contemplate the modern improvements of the place, may learn from the following quotation, what delight it was capable of imparting to this great man, before the charms of ambition had seduced him from the better occupations and sincerer pleasures of a country life. Had he never abandoned his gardens and fish-ponds, he would have died indeed a country gentleman, but probably in a good old age, and in the course of nature.

Sir Thomas Wentworth to Sir George Calvert, Principal Secretary of State.

" Our harvest is all in ; a most fine season to make fishponds ; our plums all gone and past, pearches, quinces, and grapes almost fully ripe, which will, I trow, hold better relish with a Thistleworth palate. These only we countrymen muse of, hoping in such harmless retirements for a just defence from the higher powers, and, possessing ourselves in contentment, pray with Dryope in the poet,"

" Et si qua est pietas, ab acutae falcis, et pecoris morsu frondes defendite nostrass."*

Gawthorp, August 31st, 1624.

---

*" And if there is any piety, defend our foliage from the wound of the sharp pruning hooks and from the biting of the cattle."

In the Wentworth family (says Dr. Whitaker) this beautiful estate continued during four generations; but the embarrassment which took place in the family affairs, after the death of the first Earl of Strafford, induced his son to expose the Manor of Harewood to Sale, on which occasion it was recommended to the public notice by the following advertisement, the style of which may be compared or contrasted with the puff of a modern Auctioneer.

10th Novemb. 1656.

A Particular of the Castle and Manor of Harewood, conteyneinge the Manor of Gawthorpe, and divers Lands, Tenements, and Hereditaments hereafter-mentioned; in the County of Yorke, belonging unto the Right Honourable William Earl of Strafford: The Castle decayed: the Seigniory noble, of a great extent, though formerly greater before the outparts thereof was cutt of,

———————

The Castle of Harewood decayed, yet the stones thereof being much Ashler, and the Timber that is left fit for building an hansom new house, &c. may save a deale of charges in the stonework, or els (if allowed to tenants of Harwood towne for repayers and building) would bee very usefull and necessary and serviceable for that purpose, considering it is a Market Towne therefore the Castle may be adjudged to bee well worth 30l. There is belonging to the same a very large Barne. *

There is a Charter for a Market to bee held every Munday in this Towne of Harwood, which Charter was procured † by my late Lord of Strafford about 93 years agoe, with 2 head Faires besides a fortnight faier in summer tyme, which if well managed and some money imployed in a Stock to that purpose, might bring in tyme the Market to a good height, and the houses repayred and built with the Castle Stone, which the Tenants would do at their own Charge, might much advantage the same, there being a large Toll-booth or Court-house and butchers snambles already built with 6 Shoppes under the Toll-booth for that purpose and therefore to be considered to advance the Sale.

There is a Mannor of a great extent with Court Leet and Court Baron Waives and Estrayes and fellon goods &c. belonging the same, also large Comons, the whole Lo^p. stored with all kind of wild fowle, the River of Wharfe there affording great store of fishe, as Salmon, Trout, Chevins, Cumers and Eyles.

The Lord of the Mannor being the Impropriatr. hath the presentation of the viccar to the viccaridge.

In the Grounds contained in this Particuler there is great Store of Timber Trees and wood besides the Hedgerowes and besides wood to bee left for the repayer of Houses and Mill Dames worth at least 2000l.

---

* This barn was built out of the ruins of the old Castle, it had two if not three floors for threshing in it. It was pulled down in the year 1812, the length of it was 120 feet by 50. † Probably renewed, as the original charter was granted to king John.-- See page 12.

The opinion of divers is that all the wood growing in the groundes conteined in this Particuler is worth 200l.

The Stank or Pond att Hollin hall is well stored with Carpes and Eyles.

The Stank or Pond att Gawthorp with Trout, Roch, Gudgeon and Eyles.

Gawthorp Hall most part of the Walles built with good stone and all the houses covered with Slate, and a great part of that new building, four Rooms in the ould building, all waynscotted, fyve large roomes in the new building all wainscotted, likewise and collored like wallnut tree, the matereals of which house, if sould would raise 500l. at least.

To this belongeth a Park in former tymes stored with Deere, a Parkelike place it is, and a Brook running through the middle of it, which turnes 4 payer of millstones att 2 milles.

Upon the River of Wharfe there is a Corne Mill with 2 payer of milstones, the dam of which was almost all made new the last yeare and cost unto 100l.

There is att Gawthorp a Garden and Orchards about 3 Acres in compasse, fenced round with high stone walls, the Garden towards the North side hath walles lying one above another, both the Garden and Orchard well planted with great store of fruit trees of severall kinds, which with the Dovecote and the hill before the Doore, Mr. Fox hath in lieu of 8l. part of his waiges yearly."

HAREWOOD BRIDGE.

This elegant Bridge has four noble arches, which cross the river Wharf, in the high road from Leeds to Harrogate; on the north side of which, is the Ship inn, kept by Mrs. Scott, where the traveller will meet with good accommodation. This place has long been the favourite resort of anglers, and lovers of the beautiful and picturesque. The Wheel Pit abounds with most species of the finny tribe.

In June 1753, a remarkable riot took place here; much discontent having arose, and a considerable opposition being likewise made to the turnpike act, a large body of the discontented assembled in the neighbourhood of Pudsey, headed by two brothers, of the name of Langdale.

They sent a message to Edwin Lascelles, Esq. (the late Lord Harewood) that they intended to demolish the turnpike bar, then on the north side of Harewood bridge. He accordingly prepared for their arrival. In the afternoon of the 25th of June, about three hundred men armed with swords and clubs, appeared on the top of Weardley-hill.

Mr. Lascelles being ready armed, with about eighty of his tenants and workmen upon the Bridge, saw them advancing, he marched on foot at the head of his party, and met the rioters in Mill-green, and after some skirmishing, in which, several were wounded on both sides, Mr. Lascelles took about thirty prisoners, of whom ten were committed to York Castle.

The mob was so exasperated, with the loss of

the battle, that they sent another message to Mr. Lascelles, with a threat to pull down his house, (then Gawthorp Hall) he accordingly sent for the dragoons from York, which were quartered at Harewood, and Harewood Bridge, when an express came for them to go to Leeds, and quell the tumult which had taken place in that town. A body of about five hundred men assembled in Briggate, when the proclamation against rioters was read ; but this not being regarded, a person was sent to desire all persons to shut up their shops, and keep their houses ; after which the officers sent their servants with the like caution ; but the mob continuing to break the windows and the shutters of the King's Arms Inn, and tearing up the stones of the pavement to throw at the soldiers, and having knocked down the centinel upon guard there, the drum beat to arms ; the officers gave orders to the soldiers, about twenty, to fire, which was done with powder, but this no way intimidating the mob, they fired with ball, by which eight were killed, and fifty wounded, many of whom died soon afterwards.

TALBOT HALL,

Probably took its name from the family of Talbots living here. Balshall * was likewise a noted place for being the seat of that ancient family. The land is now in the possession of Mr. Leak.—It still retains the name of Talbot Close ; it is not unlikely but what they kept a mill, as millstones and many other curiosities

* Magna Britannia.

have been found here. Here is the skeleton of an Elm-tree, which has been of a very great bulk, called the Talbot-tree.

ALWOODLEY HALL.

Alwoodley commonly called Allingley, formerly the seat of a family of that name, afterwards the estate of the Franks, then to Sir Gervase Clifton, who out-did king Henry VIII. in the number of his wives; for whereas that king had three Kates, two Nans, and one Jane; the knight had three Honourable, three Worshipful, and one Well-beloved. He died in the year 1666. Most antiently the Earl of Albemarle had three plough-lands here, held of the crown in capite, by knight's service.* The present owner, James Lane Fox, Esq. of Bramham park, who in 1817 pulled down part of the old hall, to repair his mill at Scarcroft.

The other part is now inhabited by Mr. John Midgley, a farmer. A part of the brick walls is now standing, which the fruit-trees were nailed against.

The canons of Embsey had the rent out of the mill here. Alexander de Alwoodley gave twenty-five acres and a half of land in this place, with common pasture for seven oxen, three cows, and one hundred and sixty sheep, with as much wood as the monks of Siningthwaite priory had occasion for their own proper use.

* Magna Britannia, vol. 6, p. 410.

STOCKTON ON WHARF,

Now only two farmhouses, but about the fifteenth and sixteenth centuries, it is said, here was a small village, and a chapel of ease.

The situation of Stockton is exceedingly pleasant, and commands a most extensive prospect of the distant country, finely varied by towns, villages, fields, and woods. The cathedral of York is seen distinctly at the distance of twenty miles, and the view is terminated by the mountains of Craven on the west; Hambleton hills, and the Yorkshire wolds on the north-east; limestone appears in great plenty in this place, and on the margin of Wharf quite away below Tadcaster.

Here are also found, many of the ancient domestic millstones, called querns, consisting of one circular flat stone, of about eighteen inches diameter, upon which was placed the upper stone, nearly shaped like a sugar-loaf, with a hole quite through the middle, from top to bottom; on the side was a handle fixed. The whole was placed on a cloth, and the grinder poured in the corn with one hand, and with the other turned the upper stone with a rapid motion, while the meal run out at the sides, and fell upon the cloth. This method of grinding was exceedingly tedious, and would employ two pair of hands four hours; to grind one bushel of corn.—As most of the upper stones have a piece broken off the sides of each, it is probable, they were all rendered useless, by order of the lord of each manor, after the invention of wind and water-mills.

THE RIVER WHARF.

The river Wherf, or Wharf, is said by Mr. Camden, to come from the Saxon Word, Guerf, signifying Swift; and so far it may be said to answer the description, from the many rippling streams that it affords, and being too apt, from i ts quick descent, to commit violence in its rapid course when flooded.

The water of this beautiful river Wharf, first appear on the south-east side of the mountain Cam, the alpine cenis of the road, from the northern parts of Yorkshire to Lancaster, and adjacent country.

Wharfedale is a fertile open Valley, enriched by beds of pebble limestone, these beds of limestone gravel are productive of considerable profit to the owner, and a great advantage to the adjoining lands and roads.

The whole course of this river is not less than fifty miles, computing from the first rise to its joining the river Ouse, from York, at Nun-Appleton, though the whole course of the serpentine line may greatly exceed it.

The first village on its banks is Aughtershaw, whence it passes by Debdale, Yokenthwaite, Hubberholme, Buckden, Starbottom Kettlewell,*

---

* In the Year 1686, this town and Starbottom were nearly destroyed by a tempest, with a violent flood; the situation of these towns is under a large hill, from whence the rain descended with such violence for one hour and a half, at the same time the hill on one side opening and casting up water to a prodigious height, demolishing several houses, and filling others with gravel to the chamber windows; the affrighted inhabitants fled for their lives, and the loss was computed at many thousand pounds.

Cunnistone; then to the noted Kilnsey Cragg, *
Chapel House, Treffield, Lenton, Grassington,
Burnsal, Appletreewick, Barden Tower, Bolton
Priory, and Addingham, where the country
becomes more known and cultivated.

It seems to be remarkable, that the two rivers,
Wharf and Aire, which originate nearly together,
run a sort of parallel course, and disembogue
nearly alike, should not be more allied in their
dispositions. The river Aire is so slow, that in
some parts of Craven, it seems doubtful whether
it should return to its spring, or proceed to the
sea.

The general character of the Wharf, is
beautiful transparent, lively, and variable; sometimes reposing in deep pools, at others rushing
through narrow channels, or tumbling over
ledges of rock, which exasperate its waters still
more, by a contrary inclination to the current.

The lively and impetuous Wharf, seems to
have been assisted by earthquakes, in rending
asunder the ramparts which once opposed its
passage, and in producing every where a narrow
and interrupted, but a certain channel, for its
waters. In the upper part of this river, are
many of these subterraneous excavations, several
of which appear to have been the haunts of the
ancient banditti, or the retreats of the first

---

* This projecting clift, or astonishing mass of limestone,
which stretches nearly half a mile along the valley, is
situated on the high road from Kettlewell to Skipton, and
gives the timid passenger some alarm on account of its im-
pending form. By a perpendicular line, dropped from the
highest point, its elevation was found to be one hundred
and sixty-five feet. Mr. Maude compares this cliff to
Gibralter.

inhabitants. In some of these, human bones
still remain, in the rest, those of deer and other
animals, that probably have taken refuge here
in severe weather, and perished in the snow

In many parts of Wharf, are found oaks, and
other trees, considerable for bulk, but whether
they were buried at the deluge, or cut down by
the Romans, to keep the Britons from retiring
into the woods, I cannot determine.

Wharf has long been a favourite resort of the
brethren of the cork and fly.

> " In genial spring, beneath the quiv'ring shade,
> Where cooling vapours breath along the mead,
> The patient fisher takes his silent stand,
> Intent, his angle trembling in his hand;
> With looks unmov'd, he hopes the scaly breed,
> And eyes the dancing cork, and bending reed.
> Our plenteous streams a various race supply,
> The bright-ey'd perch, with fins of Indian dye;
> The silver eel, in shining volumes roll'd;
> The yellow carp, in scales bedropp'd with gold;
> Swift trouts, diversify'd with Indian stains;
> And pikes, the tyrants of the wat'ry plains."---POPE.

FISH.

The different species of fish in Wharf, are
salmon, trout, umber or grayling, barbel, chub,
dace, gudgeon, perch, pike, lamprey, and the eel,
which is incomparable. Below Arthington, are
often caught very fine perch and pike,* and
below Thorp-arch, flounder.

The salmon in this river are seldom taken in

---

* The pike is a native English fish; but must have
been scarce in the fourteenth century, when, (says Dr.
Whitaker) thirty Jacks bought to store a pond in Craven,
cost twenty shillings.

tolerable season; above Wetherby, the trout in general are white, but very sweet; such as are red or yellow, are delicious in the months of May, June, July, and August; but the salmon smelts, which once abounded in this river, are rarely caught, a deprivation, of which the epicure as well as the angler has reason to complain, as no other fish, not even the trout, are comparable to them in point of flavour. The general disappearance of this species at present identifies them with the salmon, as it took place from the very time when the latter began to be excluded by the dams, from their usual ascent up the river at the season of spawning. A very few of the parent fish, however, perhaps the most vigorous, at the time of high floods, still continue to overleap these impediments; so that the young fry is not altogether extinct.

No river would abound with greater plenty than the river Wharf, it would vie with the Drave in Hungary, which is said to be two parts water, and one part fish, could means be devised to put them out of the reach of poachers, or those base land-otters, which have a way to take them when they run, who from the temptation of sale between the devouring places of Leeds and Harrogate, are continually using every engine to destroy the several kinds.

FINIS.

DEWHIRST, PRINTER, LEEDS.

BRITISH
16 DE 81
MUSEUM

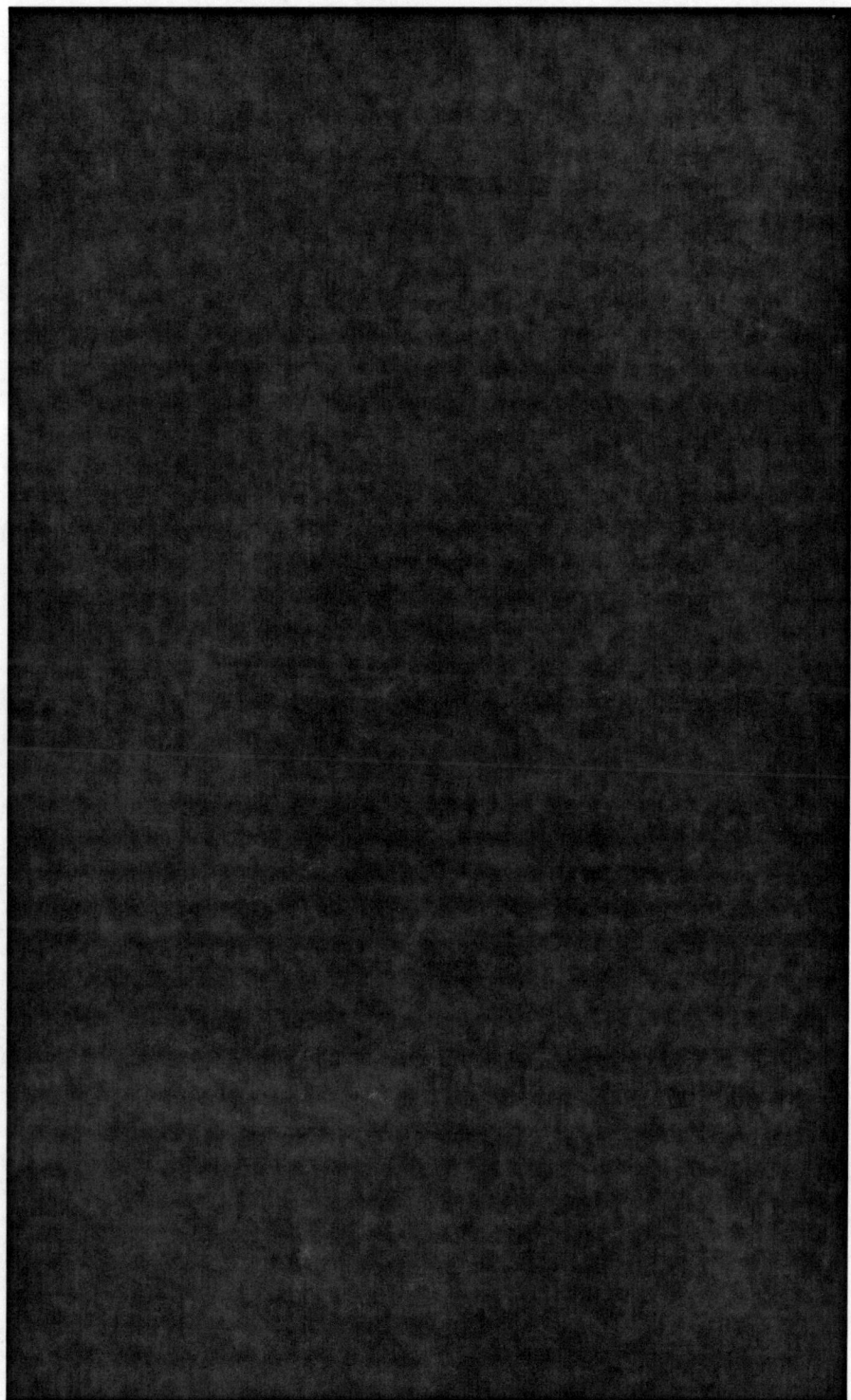

CPSIA information can be obtained
at www.ICGtesting.com
Printed in the USA
LVOW09s1704110318

569456LV00015B/331/P

9 781240 862900